THE LEAPIN'
DEACON

The Leapin' Deacon

The Soldier's Chaplain

Conrad N. Walker
and J. Walker Winslow

Foreword by
General (Ret.) John Vessey

Austin, Texas

THE LEAPIN' DEACON:
THE SOLDIER'S CHAPLAIN

CO-AUTHORS: CONRAD N. WALKER AND J. WALKER WINSLOW

Cover Graphics by Michael Qualben
Copyright © 2004 Conrad N. Walker
and J. Walker Winslow

First Printing 2004
Printed in the United States of America

Scripture quotations from *The New English Bible* © 1970
by Oxford University Press and Cambridge University Press.

PUBLISHED BY
LANGMARC PUBLISHING
P.O. 90488
Austin, Texas 78709
1-800-864-1648

Library of Congress Control Number
2004116052

ISBN: 1-880-292-920 $18.95

Dedication

To our Maker, Redeemer and Comforter be the glory.

To the Lay Leaders, Lay Ministers and Priests in the Priesthood of all Believers.

To faithful Pastors, Shepherds, Mentors—"on-the-line," in the Law and Gospel enterprises.

To Lady Ann: Cherished and loved spouse, helpmate, prayer partner, lover and friend.

To the blessed fruit of our great love, Beverly, Miriam, Randall, Timothy and Gracia, their loved spouses, our grandchildren and great grandchildren.

To Don and Bebe Walker, parents—now in heaven.

To Brother Don and Bill and families.

To the Wicinski family—Ann's family.

To J. Walker Winslow and loved wife Iva, both blessed with considerable talent and patience.

To loved and trusted Commanders, Command Sergeants Major, Officers, Non-Commissioned Officers—leaders all; and to Soldiers, Soldiers, Soldiers of all ages and ranks, a living Benediction to our Lord, Nation and Families.

Hurray for God!

Blessed to be Blessings!

CONTENTS

FOREWORD
GENERAL (RETIRED) JOHN VESSEY

"Rub-a-dub, dub, thanks for the grub. Yeah, God!"

The date was a Saturday sometime in late 1971 or early 1972. The place was the apartment my family was occupying in Bangkok during the time that my duty station was Laos.

I was in Bangkok for a Saturday night and Sunday with my family, but much of my mind was still in Laos where we were having a very difficult time with a major North Vietnamese offensive. I felt somewhat guilty being in Bangkok, but at the same time, my family had been promised that I would see them once a month, and the last visit had been more than three months earlier.

At our house, we took turns leading the table prayer. That evening, David, age thirteen, was to lead the prayer. What the Lord and the rest of us got was, "Rub-a-dub...."

My reaction was a stern countenance and a gruff, "David, where in the world did you get that?" The answer was, "Chaplain Walker taught it to me." Daughter Sarah, age sixteen, immediately chimed in with, "Dad, we think it's a wonderful prayer." After a little reflection, and pulling the remainder of my mind out of the war in Laos, so did I.

Since those days, Chaplain Connie and I have had many years of association in all sorts of circumstances from very stressful to fun-filled. Whatever the circumstances, always at the heart of Connie Walker's contribution was the exhilarating joy in the Gospel message of the Risen Lord.

That joy was present whether Connie was ministering to soldiers in the throes of battle, pastoring a senior commander with overwhelming responsibilities, or just helping a young thirteen-year-old deal with the fact that he had seen his father very infrequently in the previous five years.

Being a military chaplain has some similarities to being a pastor in a civilian community, but not many. For the military chaplain, about seventy-five percent of his parishioners are between the ages of eighteen and twenty-four. Eighty-five percent are male (and for most of Chaplain Walker's time, it was ninety-five percent). The primary occupation for one hundred percent of the parishioners is engaging in or supporting violence. When the Nation asks them to do the job they're prepared to do, death and severe injury are ever-present dangers for both parishioners and pastor alike.

When God tapped Conrad Walker to be a pastor, He clearly had the ministry to soldiers in the plan. Connie was reared on a farm, was a Golden Gloves boxing champion and a pro-quality college football player, always courageous with a great sense of humor, yet a humble man of great faith.

It would be difficult to find a better model for chaplain to combat soldiers than Connie Walker.

Chaplain Connie's story is a great story. I'm sure you'll enjoy it as much as I have enjoyed and been helped by the years of our association and friendship. For me, being near Connie Walker, whether in person, or through a letter or a phone conversation, has always reaffirmed that the good news of the Gospel, really is good news, not just good news, but the ultimate in joyous, good news!

When I'm listening to a long, drawn out, pre-dinner prayer that seems more like a sermon to the audience rather than a prayer to God, I often smile and think "Rub-a-dub, dub, thanks for the grub. Yeah, God!" might be more appropriate.

General (Retired) John (Jack) Vessey
Former Chairman of the Joint Chiefs of Staff

PREFACE

Dateline: Jungles near Xuan Loc, Vietnam-29 June 1966

"As the relief force entered our area, Chaplain Connie Walker was the first man to reach me. I was in tears; I had lost some of the best fighting men in the world. Many of my boys, I knew, would never fight for their country again. I tried to show the chaplain the most severely wounded, but he realized our state of mind and immediately had prayer with me, then went to every man. While praying with PFC William Marshall of Detroit, he noticed that the young soldier was bleeding heavily above the tourniquet on his arm, which had been blown off below the elbow.

Chaplain Walker used part of his own clothing and quickly applied another tourniquet high on the arm and stopped the bleeding.

After rendering spiritual aid, the chaplain started chopping trees to try and clear an LZ for the evacuation of the wounded and dead. I've never seen a man in my life work as hard as he did. The chaplain is a 'mighty big man'. He seemed to be a tower of strength. Every time that my vision cleared so that I could see, I saw him working like a buzz saw. He even held huge trees as they were being chopped down, using a 'bear hug' and moved them to avoid hitting our wounded comrades. I could never express the respect and appreciation Chaplain Walker won that bloody day."

SGT Charles B. Morris
—Medal of Honor Recipient

Introduction I

by J. Walker Winslow

Everything about Conrad N. "Connie" Walker is unique and extraordinary. Consequently, I find no fault with his written biography being a bit the same.

Hi! I'm J. Walker Winslow, and although I call myself a writer, I've never before been involved with a book. Under normal circumstances, I'm a humor and a travel writer. It happens, however, that ever so often in the literary world, a person comes along that somehow rings-one's-bell, so to speak, and interests a writer so much, that he can't continue with his ordinary activity until this new distracting "itch" is scratched.

Connie has become my "itch."

Ideally this should be an autobiography—and really it is. I'm just along for the ride. If the world waited until Connie Walker had time to do it, however, it would never get done. So, it is co-written.

If things had worked out just a bit differently, I might be recording about Connie Walker, former heavyweight contender for the World Boxing Crown, or even Connie Walker, former professional NFL football star lineman. The opportunities were there and the recruiters lined up as Connie left the University of Washington. It seems that God got in the way.

Connie didn't succumb to the siren's song sung by the pro football ranks or the lure of the potentially lucrative life of the heavyweight-boxing world. He entered Luther Seminary instead in St. Paul, Minnesota, and at about the same time, he joined the Minnesota National Guard.

On the surface of things, these two happenings seem a bit unrelated and rather ordinary. Forty years later, Leon VanAutreve, retired Sergeant Major of the Army (the top enlisted position attainable), told me, "The Chaplaincy should establish a 'Hall of Fame' and Connie Walker should be one of the first inducted." (Sergeant Major VanAutreve went home to be with the Lord while this book was being compiled. We were blessed for knowing him.)

Am I qualified to be the recorder of this extraordinary "Viking Chaplain's" story? Probably not, but I am, however, so blessed.

I met Connie over a decade ago at the twilight of his glorious military career. It was also the beginning of his continuing ministry. Tens of hundreds had already experienced life-altering relationships with him—the legend was firmly in place.

There's that word again. One thing that I was not prepared for, as I started this project, was the number of times I heard of Connie referred to as a "legend" and yet, time and again this was the tag used to describe him by many of the dozens of responses that I have had from all over the world about this remarkable gentleman.

Another thing the reader of this chronology of a spiritual hero might become accustomed to are the number of quotes from relatives, admirers, mentees, and those who Connie lovingly refer to as his "Pups." No need to count them, however, as there will be a long line of them to greet you at the gates of Heaven.

To fully appreciate Connie's story, one must embrace his entire life, the Alpha to the Omega, the beginning to the not-yet-accomplished end. We will look at the materialistically Spartan years; the effect of hard-earned education; the inspiration of early ministry; the well-deserved glory of a military career—and the beauty of the continuing ministry.

We will be allowed a glimpse of each era. We will meet scores of family and friends, mentors and mentees, comrades and, in some cases, hear of the life changes brought by knowing this "giant of a man."

To spend more time on what the following pages are going to do would become self-serving and redundant.

Therefore, I invite you—gentle reader—to accompany me on this journey—this adventure.

The reader may notice that the first four chapters are presented as information from me to you, pretty much as Connie (and others) related the information to me. From about the military years and following, we listen more to Connie directly, with comments and notes from me when Connie for one reason or another didn't elaborate (or his natural modesty held him back).

Make no mistake, although I am the one recording the words, Conrad Norman Walker is the one that God blessed with this extraordinary life. There are thousands of Christian souls that have benefited from having come in contact with this Soldier's Chaplain, this Leapin' Deacon, this Man of God.

As the journey of thousands of miles begins, we are in rural Illinois—the Depression Years as Don Dougal and Bebe Walker welcome their second son, a son who would one day be remembered as "The Leapin' Deacon —The Soldier's Chaplain."

Well, now you know why I'm involved and how, but I said earlier that you might find this book a bit unique.

So how about starting with a second introduction—one from the man himself? How about it Connie?

J. Walker Winslow

INTRODUCTION II
by Conrad N. Walker

Dear Readers and Friends, People of God and Friends of God:

Grace and Peace to you from God, our Father, our Lord Jesus Christ and the powerful and winsome Holy Spirit.

Life is a splendid and adventuresome journey and pilgrimage of Faith, along with a bold and sure sense of being "called and sent." As one considers the journey of life and ministry over the past decades, I am captured by a joyous thanksgiving, but at the same time, clearly declare that I am not the good, but thanks be to God, the *forgiven*! As a forgiven sinner, life is packed with hope, fun and jubilance. We are the called ones. We are the sent ones by God's grace, mercy and glory to his exalted mission.

Let us prayerfully celebrate high adventure living and continue to "Walk the walk" and go forth under His commission as forgiven truth-tellers.

I profoundly rejoice in the friendship and witness of the superb and gifted humor and travel writer, J. Walker Winslow. He is a blessing par-excellence as we labor and work together on this journey of faith, hope, and love.

Truly, we are "on our way rejoicing."

Conrad (Connie) N. Walker

Chapter 1

"Humor is the Harmony of the Heart"
Douglas Jerrold: 1803-1857

Joshua 24:15. ". . . But I and my family, we will serve the Lord."-NEB

Dateline: Herrick, Illinois—2 March 1932. "And in this corner, weighing in at eleven pounds even, wearing no trunks at all, and making his initial appearance in the arena-of-life, **Conrad Norman Walker**."

Facetious? Perhaps. It is also appropriate to introduce—in a vein of humor—this blessed Child of God. One destined to become a star athlete, a beloved young pastor, a legendary chaplain and heroic soldier, as well as an inspirational speaker, mentor and truth teller.

Even to the day these words are written, Connie (as he is known to most) teaches and preaches to pastors and laypersons alike to maintain a strong element of humor in their ministry. "You'll be glad you did," he tells them, and then continues to walk-the-walk.

Please Meet Connie's Early Family

It is nearly impossible to become acquainted with Connie's early years (or his entire life for that matter) without first recognizing his immediate, and extended, family. Family is—and has been from day one—an integral part of the whole that is Connie Walker, and it is improbable that one could understand fully the one without the other.

This writer has come to picture the Walker family (Connie's dad's side) and the Hagen family (Connie's mom's side) as the equivalent to Siamese twins: only, rather than being joined at the hip, they are joined at the spirit.

Don Dougal Walker (Dad). Don Dougal Walker: stalwart citizen of Herrick, Illinois. An eighth-grade "drop-out," who would often be described by those who knew him as "one of the wisest men I know." A contractor by trade, a lifetime of wrestling wheelbarrows full of concrete had developed a hearty six-footer, built (as Connie would later describe), "of a sturdy and impressive frame."

Two things shaped much of Don Dougal's life: his love of history and a lifelong admiration for a fellow Illinois citizen, Abraham Lincoln. Oh yes, there was one more thing, a credo he adhered to all of the days of his life—*"Whatever you do, do well. Whatever you start—finish."*

"Our father was the primary influence in our leading unselfish lives. He had an absolute view of doing what was 'right' by *his* definition. He believed in everybody having a chance. Education was emphasized as the highest priority. While he saw it as the way to a better life for his sons, he also saw it as a quality-of-life issue. Education enhanced the whole of life."—William "Bump" Walker (third son of three)

Bodvild "Bebe" Walker née Hagen (Mom). Bebe Hagen arrived in the United States as a seventeen-year-old immigrant from (in Connie's words), "The majestically beautiful country of Norway." She was accompanied by Ole Hagen, her father, and Norman Hagen, her brother, and in her possession (this becomes very significant) three books: The Word of God (Bible), the Lutheran Catechism, and a hymnal.

Even though Bebe was a strikingly beautiful lady, it was her remarkable strength of character, complementing Don Dougal's own, that would have such a profound influence on the Walker generation yet to come. Like Don Dougal, Bebe was very limited in education, but she was an avid reader. She developed near perfect English on her own and fostered a learning environment in her home. No sacrifice was too great for the advantage of her family; the added benefit, "What a great cook!" (Consensus of the Walker boys.)

Cynthia "Cindy" Walker (grandmother). A true matriarch. A half century later, Connie would remember her as "a mighty person of prayer." If the stability of a structure, a project, or yes, a family, depends on a solid foundation, one needs look no further than Grandma Cindy. Again and again, while discussing the Walker family and Connie's early years, one name (besides Don Dougal and Bebe) is a constant reference: "Our saintly Grandma Cindy."

There is a thread of commonality that flows throughout this entire adventure, and the fibers of that thread are several fold: Family values, a deep sense of personal responsibility, and a profound acceptance of Christian spirituality. The headwater of that flow is most certainly—Grandma Cindy.

Ole Hagen (Connie's maternal grandfather). At six foot four and about three hundred pounds (also a bit of a rascal), we shall see that Ole (Connie's godfather as well) played a significant role in Connie's early years.

A remarkable early life as a member of Norway's Royal Guard, he moved rather nicely into a fine education and a career as a civil engineer. All of this ended rather abruptly, due to a lapse of good judgment—and a bit of larceny. These actions prompted a rather hasty immigration to the United States in the late 1920s. Ole eventually settled in the Chicago area with one son, Norman, and one lovely daughter, Bebe, in tow.

Roy "Tuffy" Walker (uncle). Brother to Don Dougal, Roy made a lasting impression on the Walker boys. He was probably an inspiration for the two oldest boys' lifelong interest (and excellence) in boxing.

A strong-willed, able-bodied and yet lovable man of character, he is remembered even to this day as one whose "Yes was yes, and his no was no." The other thing that Uncle Tuffy was known for was fighting at the drop of a hat. He was never known to lose either a hat or a fight.

Pearl and "Bing" Crosby (aunt and uncle). Grandma Cindy's daughter Pearl and Pearl's husband, Byron (Bing), are beautiful persons on the inside and the outside. They have been lifelong encouragers, advisors, prayer partners, and bold witnesses to our Lord Jesus. They remain forever a blessing and inspiration to the Walker boys.

Norman Hagen (uncle). Norman was truly a stalwart Norwegian/American hero. He served as a combat engineer in General George Patton's 3rd Army in WWII. He inspired the entire family with his many letters from the dangerous combat zone. He encouraged the family to "Keep the faith, and pass it on." He created special joy when he brought home his beautiful British war bride, Connie's Aunt Madge. She was an officer in the British Army as a nurse. She remains a powerful influence in the lives of the Walker family as a mighty person of prayer and as a Bible study leader. God must be praised for her!

Don Walker (brother). Blessed brother Don, eighteen months Connie's senior, was destined to become one of the church's strongest ministers in his part of the Midwest. Being the eldest sibling, the task of shepherding the young rambunctious Connie during the toddler and formative years fell to Don's husky shoulders—no small task.

Don, outstanding athlete, patriot, and journeyman businessman, would take several paths on life's road, prior to following Connie's example of ministering to God's children. He has remained to this day as much of a hero to Connie as Connie is to him.

William Walker (brother). Seven years Connie's junior, William "Bump" Walker, stood in the shadow of his older brothers' accomplishments and, at the same time, emitted a brilliant light of his own. Bill became one of Minnesota's leading District Court Judges. He has maintained the Walker Mantra—"Whatever you do, do well, and whatever you start, finish." (And then some!) Bill is a true American leader and a trusted friend.

Connie would have us know one of the many hardships overcome by God and family in the early days of brother Bill.

"Bill could not take our dear mother's milk, or store bought milk, or formula," Connie said. "We all became deeply worried as brother Bill was not doing well. A wise country doctor came on the scene and said to Dad, 'Don, right away, get a couple of milk goats.' It worked marvelously. Brother Bill flourished nicely, and we were blessed in learning other skills—how to milk goats, care for them, and keep them healthy and producing. The entire family leaped with joy, as Bill became strong, very active, and full of smiles. I heard Dad walking around the outside of the little two-room home saying, 'Thank you, Lord, thank you, Jesus.' His heart spoke deeply as he was ever so well taught by Grandma Cindy."

CHAPTER 2

IN THE BEGINNING

Psalm 100:5. "For the Lord is good; his steadfast love endures forever, and his faithfulness to all generations."-NEB

I Peter 1:3-5. Praise be to the God and Father of our Lord Jesus Christ, who in his great mercy gave us new birth into a living hope by the resurrection of Jesus Christ from the dead! The inheritance to which we are born is one that nothing can destroy...It is kept for you in heaven..."-NEB

As mentioned, Bebe was a teenage immigrant from the majestic and picturesque country of Norway. Don Dougal, however, was a native of Herrick, Illinois, which gives us a launching pad for Connie's early years.

Herrick is located in south-central Illinois. It is a small village north of Vendalia and south of Decatur. Emphasis is placed on this bit of geography because of things yet to come. It is worthy also of mention that this was the height of the Great Depression and a time of intense economic poverty. Pointed emphasis on materialism—why?

In Connie's words, "Mother was most desirous that her three sons be baptized and convinced. She would have that they be taught the wondrous Word of God and be in covenant relationship to our great God, Redeemer Jesus, and friend, the Holy Spirit."

With this daily influence and welcomed associations with Grandma Cindy (she of never-ending faith), the Walker boys were assured the most fortuitous grounding in parental spirituality.

Don Dougal epitomized (and insisted upon) hard and steady work as part of daily life: everything from working the always present garden, to carrying water, to going into the surrounding forest to cut (with ax and crosscut saw) and carry in the wood, to stacking the firewood neatly. This was for daily use and in preparation for the coming colder and, oft times, severe winter.

Later, work would include helping the family subsist with hunting and trapping. Even later, as boys doing men's work, there would be the concrete business and even a fledgling garbage business.

The stringent work ethic from the earliest days produced in the Walker boys hard, firm, and resilient bodies, which would serve each of them well over the course of their lifetimes. We'll see examples of this again and again in athletics, academics, business, military, social involvement, and most notably in ministry of God's Holy Word (for Don and Connie). Bill was cut from the same loaf but a different slice. With this degree of wealth of family, of what importance is materialism?

It is interesting to note that, other than the emotional security engendered by the closeness of this idealistic family, the earliest memories of all three boys deal with food. Connie reminisces, "I clearly remember early on smells and aromas of housecleaning and seasonal preparation for Advent, Christmas, the Lenten season, and

Easter. But oh, that most cherished joyful smell was of mother's baking of bread, biscuits, and some special goodies for her boys, neighbors, and friends."

Brother Don adds, "Grandma Cindy was a poor widow who had raised her children and considered herself rich for her family and the Lord's grace giving her all she needed for a living. The little lady could catch and kill chickens as fast as anyone that I've ever seen, because her family had come and she was going to feed them. How delicious her preparations...with biscuits and milk gravy, fresh vegetables from the garden, and scrumptious bacon and ham from her own hog."

"Poverty would be a word that could describe most of our years as a family," Bill says. "It was serious poverty. Yet, with that reality, we never were wanting for medical attention or food. Our father was a survivor first class, and our mother a cook of the first order. He raised much of our food and, while our parents may not have always gotten the medical attention *they* needed, *we* did." (*JWW note:* These memories are as vivid fifty or sixty years later as originally. Important? You bet!)

Home is Where the Work is

For many, perhaps even most, people, the Great Depression was characterized by a continual scramble for survival. As naturally talented as was Don Dougal Walker, he was no exception.

Sometime before Connie's birth in 1932, the Walker family had established themselves for a time in the Long Lake area of northern Illinois just north of Chicago, some two hundred miles from Herrick. There were two sound reasons for having migrated there: one, Don Dougal was able to find enough work to feed his family, and two, Grandpa Ole Hagen had established himself in the fish business in Chicago. The significance of this location will become apparent later on in Connie's formative years, but first his brother Don has some memories for us.

Don seems to remember the family returning to Herrick shortly before Connie's arrival, probably prompted by the work situation and the fact that Grandma Cindy was adept at aidin' birthin'.

"The earliest thoughts I have of Conrad that I believe were of that time, or soon after, were at his birth," Don says. "It was in the living room of Grandma Cindy's. I know I was young enough to be embraced by her as she sat in a rocking chair with her arms wrapped around me saying, 'Thank you, Jesus! Thank you, Jesus!' I think it could certainly have been her giving praise to God for mother's deliverance and Connie's birth.

"The situation is really cloudy, but the words from my grandmother are clear and being on her lap is vivid. She was a small lady, so I could not have been too big, near the age of eighteen months, when my brother was born.

"This time instills in my mind as one of the main plantings of God's Word that I remember . . . as it came from my grandmother. She was a devout Pentecostal Christian, whose love and embrace permeates my life and my brother's. From her, I heard about Jesus in our earliest of all memories, just as it had to be Connie's even earlier experience, for he was born in her living room on March 2, 1932."

Don adds, as only an older brother can, "I somehow remember that Connie wasn't the prettiest baby, but then to an older brother, I suppose anyone, boy or girl, isn't pretty. After all, I was the king of the roost—the firstborn of the family—and had been the center of attention. Now I had to share it. Sibling rivalry has something to do with character building, both bad and good.

"Connie's roots undeniably are there as much as any place, I believe, first because of his birth, but secondly because of his faith early on hearing up front and right off the platter about Jesus Christ, His power, and His love. Thinking about it has given me cause to say this, as if I never really put that all together the same way.

"I do know, for both of us, that Grandma Cindy was a most positive influence to knowing Jesus up close, as if in His own arms and embrace. Her faith rubbed off on all of us through her deep, loving eyes and firm, caring hands, and her busy little body running in and out of the house getting a meal together for everybody—a feast! I don't remember having anything at her house that was not like a feast, even breakfast—or *especially* breakfast."

The task of "riding herd" on the rambunctious young Connie fell to the sturdy shoulders of older brother Don. This was no easy task for, even then, Connie seemed in constant motion. This would prove to be so for *all* the preschool years and beyond, no matter where home might be.

So it was that as equally important as moving the family to Herrick for Connie's birth, the time soon came for reasons of livelihood to head for the Long Lake region.

Back to the North

As comforting as it may have been in Herrick (with Grandma Cindy's spiritual strength and open door for family), Long Lake, Illinois offered more opportunity for Don Dougal to care for his family. There was ample foliage for productive hunting and trapping. There were also more people that could use the many tradesman talents that Don Dougal possessed.

It was also a good area for two vigorous toddlers to stretch their legs and grow in the physical mold of their father and the spiritual vision of their mother. The years to come would be favorably impacted by the stringent learning process now in motion.

The Great Candy Bar Caper

One incident during this toddler age well deserves telling. It marks well the degree of zest with which Connie approaches life, and it points out vividly the degree of competitiveness Connie has displayed all of his days.

As Spartan and fiscally difficult as was the depth of the Great Depression, Don Dougal did everything in his power to give his family as normal and happy a life as possible. To this end, he was able to come by a much-appreciated tricycle for his dear boys to use.

Connie would spend many hours on the walks and paths with this prized possession. One day, Don Dougal was pleased that he could bring his boys a wonderful and infrequent treat: a chocolate candy bar for each of them, and oh my goodness there was a delicious marshmallow center—surely a blessing from above!

Connie decided to enjoy this delectable boon while exploring the oft-traveled walks aboard his leg-powered mode of transportation. What could be more perfect? It was a beautiful day, and he was in possession of a luscious gift from his dad.

Connie didn't expect, however, the neighbor's dog suddenly appearing and purloining Connie's chocolate treasure. The neighbor's dog didn't expect Connie on his tricycle chasing him down, bull-dogging him as deftly as a rodeo champion, and biting him on the ear until the unscrupulous felon gave up the candy bar and rapidly vacated the area. Not surprisingly, the dog never tried that again.

Thank you, Mighty Lord and Protector!

This writer would be remiss if I omitted one story that occurred at an even earlier date. It was a day when Connie was a bit past his second birthday. In hindsight, it's easy to see that had things turned out differently, thousands of people would have been adversely affected in the years to follow.

"Brother Don was and remains a most kindly and patient person," Connie says. "He carefully watched after me for days on end. One bright morning, however, I set out alone on a secret journey to check out the entire area. Our home was surrounded on three sides by water. I soon disappeared in the water and was drowning.

"Grandpa Hagen was out on his morning walk and observed the channel water churning a bit. He came over to look and saw me on the bottom of three feet of water. This strapping Viking immediately jumped into the water, pulled me to safety, and using first-aid, he restored my breathing—indeed, saving my life.

"Grandpa Hagen was both my Godfather at holy baptism and my rescuer on that day. He was also a clear and bold witness to the Lordship of Jesus Christ. Brother Don remained on the job, as difficult as it was, watching after his robust younger brother and allowing Mother and Dad to go about their work and chores. He was and is a most loving, effective and remarkable man in a vast arena of skills. Praise God."

Those early days in Long Lake are dear to the two older Walker boys and played an important part in impressing upon them the importance of family unity. These are lifelong values that have been passed to additional generations, now some sixty-plus years later.

Back to the South

In difficult times, the Walker family always adjusted to what was best for the family, considering the circumstances at the time. That meant once again relocating to Herrick. Connie would attend his first two years of school in the village of his birth.

Here also was dear Grandma Cindy and her unshakable faith, never-ending energy, and an extraordinary capacity for love and kindness.

Another trait shared by the entire Walker family is a boundless thirst for knowledge. This was evident with Bebe's huge appetite for reading and her development of near-perfect, self-taught English. Don Dougal's interest in history was also a lifelong quest.

It isn't surprising, therefore, that all of the Walker boys were accomplished readers at an early age. With the influence of both Cindy and Bebe, that meant the Holy Bible was an oft-read and well-referenced text in the family.

Highlighting one story that is particularly dear to his heart, Connie says, "I recall that when I could first read, Grandma Cindy would call to me, 'Connie, get in here and read to me. I can't see or hear too well, so you have at it for me. Read loud and clear.' She would usually have me begin in the book of Psalms—what a beautiful choice and a way of prayer for us, as the book of Psalms is indeed God's prayer book!

"She would then follow with, 'Read the Gospel of John, the first chapter. Real loud and real clear—you know, like a pastor does.' Then she would guide me to Romans 8. Wow! What a wise and humorous way she would use to get the Word of God into the hearts and minds of grandchildren."

Brother Don Remembers those Years

About those years just before Connie started school, Don vividly remembers, "We lived in poor times. Everyone worked and pitched in to make things go. Our dad worked very hard and long, doing whatever he could to have food on the table. I remember that he made about $35 a month as a policeman and another $35 a month tending a large herd of goats. Whatever else he did was by the job here and there as a jack-of-all-trades. He was a mighty knowledgeable man about doing things, and he took the time to show his boys how. He then expected us to remember and do what he'd taught us."

In regard to Connie, Don adds, "I want to inject this here because somehow it was an undeniable factor in our relationship from early on. I think Connie and I always loved each other—not to our credit—but by the fact that we had no choice. There was bound to be tension and animosity between siblings, but the rule of the house from Dad was, 'You must *not* fight. If you want to fight, we'll have you put the gloves on, and I will referee. If you fight, then you both get a lickin', then I'll know I got the right one.' That was a rule written in stone. We got a few lickins' that we long remembered. For the most part, however, we got along and had a deep respect for each other as well."

Don Dougal had another cardinal rule of the house, according to brother Don. "Don't get into trouble at school." He taught this rule to the boys in graphic fashion.

On Connie's first day of school, Don walked with his two boys rather than letting them take the bus. He wanted to meet the principal. With the boys alongside, the conversation went something like this, "Hello, Mr. Kennel. I'm Don Walker and these are my boys, Don and Conrad. I want you to know, Mr. Kennel, that if they need it, you have my permission to give them a lickin'. The only thing I ask is that you let me know so as they will get one when they get home, too."

Don reminisced that they knew it didn't pay to get into trouble at school, so quite frankly, they didn't.

Grandma Cindy Makes a Lasting Impression

About the time that Connie was to enter the second grade in the small grade school in Herrick, Grandma Cindy did one of those small neat things that one remembers all of one's days.

During the warmer summer months, the Walker boys generally went barefoot no matter what they were doing, be it chores or playtime.

"As the school year was rushing in on us," Connie said, "I was given a pair of hand-me-down shoes with a big hole in the sole of one shoe that was home repaired with a strong piece of cardboard until replacements could be purchased.

"Grandma Cindy paid a visit to encourage us for the forthcoming schooling and classes. Seeing my shoes, she said, 'Connie, let's go into town. I've got several things to do and to purchase.' We walked to town and right to the shoe store, and she purchased a pair of tennis shoes.

"Connie," she said, "these will aid your walking and running, and I notice that you like to run and are quick. It was a kind and most helpful gift from a dear and godly Grandma Cindy at a most strategic time in life. Praise God."

A Blessing from God and Another from Dad

Two other happenings during Connie's first two years of school made lasting impressions. The first and foremost was the addition of the third Walker son. William Walker, seven years Connie's junior, was welcomed on the scene. The blessings of God are without end.

The second is a fine example of priorities being in the right place. Both Don and Connie relate the following as the best Christmas gift they received as youngsters.

"At a young age," Don said, "we had to learn to work, starting with chores: feed the pigs and chickens (though Mother did a lot of that), and feed and milk the cow. We learned early on how to saw and gather wood. That was our responsibility.

"One special Christmas present neither of us would ever forget: Dad got us a two-man crosscut saw. Connie was eight years old and I was about nine and a half. We were so glad to have that saw, because previously everything had to be cut up with an axe or a small Swiss saw. Yes, we indeed lived in poor times."

CHAPTER 3

THE LIGHT GOES ON

Proverbs 22:6. "Start a boy on the right road, and even in old age, he will not leave it."-NEB

Prayer by Lyman Beecher: "God grant that our principal men shall be men of principle."

A study of the life of Conrad N. Walker brings the realization that it would be a disservice to the reader if an attempt were made to weigh one era as more important than any other in the embodiment of his whole person. Yet . . .

Surely, the events between first grade and high school were as telling in the development of character for this stalwart child of God as any in his storied life.

Three influences (plus one more to be introduced in the short chapter following this one) were responsible for the remarkable evolvement of this young, blessed and destined man during this era. The first was family influence.

Eric Berne (1910-1970; founder of Transactional Analysis) taught that our lives are pre-ordained from childhood by what he called scripts. A script is the parental/ancestral blueprint for an individual's life, much like the blueprint that a builder follows when constructing a house.

It is from our parents that we learn how to think for ourselves or how not to, how to have relationships or how not to, and how to succeed or how to live a life of quiet desperation.

In other words, our parents' behaviors, choices, and attitudes model and shape our childhood perceptions, world views and beliefs. Each of us then lives out countless "shoulds" which, if not evaluated as adulthood approaches, can cripple our zest for living, thwart our ability to know what we want to do with our lives, and render us impotent in matters of creative, independent thinking.

The point has already been made about the importance *of* and the appreciation *for* both the immediate and the extended family unit that is this remarkable clan. Yet, not too much emphasis can be placed on the lasting effect that the shared closeness and respect experienced by the Walker boys has had. The effect is not only on them, but on all who have come into contact with them as well, even to the day of this writing.

The tough love and even-handed discipline and standard-setting role provided by Don Dougal Walker had a lasting effect on each of the Walker boys in every aspect of their lives. The sons were well aware that in this family, "Yes was yes, and no was no."

The lessons were learned well: respect, responsibility, and appreciation for jobs well done and the kind of love that can only come from honest and caring people. Connie states, "The law and gospel, faith life, deep character-producing and value-producing settings were always the first order in our home." Truth telling was the order of the day in the Walker home.

It is in the spirit of truth telling that Connie would have us know that everything just written was not always idyllic. There was a time (especially during Connie's late teenage years) when, in Connie's words, "Father at times had his nose too far into the suds." This was to be a bone of contention between father and son for some time until finally, through the grace of God, the problem was resolved.

It is definitely so with Connie, and I suspect with his brothers as well, that when speaking of their mother Bebe, a loving smile crosses the face and a certain tenderness comes over them.

"Within the clear guidelines for our family life," Connie says, "there was considerable warmth, affirmation, and love displayed by both parents. However, it was particularly shown by our Norwegian mother. She was a worker par excellence in and outside of the home. She would clean homes for other families, she waited tables at a local dining facility; she even had her own café called Bebe's in Long Lake." All of this was at the time of Connie's late elementary school and early high school years in Fox Lake (Ingleside), Illinois.

During that cluster of years, Connie remembers his mother working in a shag rug factory in nearby Libertyville, Illinois—always assisting, always helping—always pressing hard to make ends meet in the home. "Plus she was a good home keeper," Connie says, "as I've often noted with fond memory, baking bread and biscuits and other creative goodies."

All three of the Walker boys seem to remember this period of Connie's early schooling with great clarity and fondness. One of Connie's shared memories is the fact that the one extended period of sickness that he recalls in his life (other than military injuries, years later) occurred during the third grade. Connie missed so much school time that he was required to repeat the third grade—a happening that Connie would see for the rest of his life as a blessing from God.

During 1939-1940—particularly austere and frugal years for the Walkers—Don Dougal impressed upon the two older boys (since brother Bill was just arriving on the scene) a seemingly apparent, yet important declaration. "I can give you only the one big gift of 'desire.' I'll build your bodies up in strength on the cement gang. However, you cannot count on Mom and me to send you to college or university. You must use your minds, hearts, and desire on the athletic field (for grant-in-aid scholarships) to do it." Steadfastness in family traditions, inner and outer strength, and the desire to do their best was built into Don Dougal's gift.

Brother Don Remembers

Connie's big brother Don has become one of the foremost Lutheran pastors in the Midwest. It didn't start out that way, however. During his lifetime, Don has been an outstanding athlete, businessman, served a two-year stint in the Navy, and has been well recognized by many for his avocation of general craftsman extraordinaire. Oh yes, and one more thing—along with brother Bill, Don was one of Connie's best friends.

"Connie and I enjoyed doing things together; in fact, much of the time we were each other's only playmates during early childhood. About the time Connie started school, a third boy was also in the family, our young brother, Bill. We lived in a small, two-room house with a dug well right outside the front door, and the outhouse was out back.

"Connie and I slept on a mattress in the attic. One morning after a snowstorm, we woke up and there was a layer of snow on the blanket, so the roof was not in very good shape. None of the house was in very good shape. We didn't know it then—it was home to us—and even though the house wasn't much, we were blessed time after time with loving care and nourishment by our parents."

Brother Don furnishes another insight to Connie's character during those early years with the toboggan story.

"Once, when Connie was about eleven years old, we were sledding on a hill just about a mile from our home when our loaded toboggan was headed for a line of trees. Connie tried as hard as he could to steer the toboggan away from the trees, to no avail.

"In a last-ditch attempt, he slid off of the sled. Using his body as a brake, he managed to stop the impending accident. In the process, a branch off a tree impaled his buttock, penetrating about the size and length of a big finger. We ran and pulled him home as quickly as we could, and I remember the feeling of panic. As I remember it, however, Connie kept his composure more than any of us did all the way home. As bad as it was, without his actions, it could have been a lot worse."

Up to the age of about sixteen, Connie and his brother Don worked closely with their dad, as Don Dougal tried different work wherever work was available. He did the water well business. He did the septic tank business. He twice tried the tavern business and went broke both times, but he was successful in the gravel and cement construction business.

"Connie and I learned what it is to dig and to make cement," Don said. "There were no backhoes that we knew of. In those days, we were the backhoes. Connie and I know how to dig, if we know nothing else in this life. Dad prided himself in our work when he looked down a 100 foot of drainage field, 1 foot wide and 4 foot deep, and said 'my boys can dig the straightest ditch there is.' He was right."

As the recorder of all the testimonies given for this undertaking, I was struck by the fact that all three brothers vividly recalled and related one incident in particular that had occurred when Connie was about fifteen years of age—a full fifty-five years prior to this writing.

Using younger brother Bill's words (although they are almost all identical with his two brothers' words), "I remember sitting on our front porch with Mom and Dad. We heard a loud noise coming from the lumberyard a block away where Don and Connie both worked. Dad ran up there. Soon I saw my brothers, both were very big men, walking home with heads down and Dad spanking them all the way with a willow stick. They had gotten into a fight with each other. It was then that I learned what the concept of family meant. In our house, brother did not fight brother. It was an *uncommon* behavior prior to this and *unheard* of behavior after."

"While working together as brothers," Don recalls, "one of my fond memories is starting a business. Together with Dad, we decided to establish a garbage removal service. We lived where most homes were on the lake as places of summer vacationing. There was no sanitation service in the area. So our dad provided a 1936 Ford dump truck on which we put high sideboards. Into this, the garbage cans and other refuse was manually lifted, dumped, and then stomped down by foot. We were literally in the garbage business!

"The enterprise grew immediately to over one hundred customers—and kept growing. We did very well for two high school kids. Later on, after Connie and I had gone on to college, Dad sold the route for what he thought was a fair price. However, the business was then sold (not much later) for ten times the amount that he received. Today of course, it is a major enterprise.

"In all of these experiences (more than I can remember), all of us learned a lot of things. It was our job and duty toward our family. There wasn't any time I can remember when there wasn't work that needed to be done. It wasn't hardship; it was just the way it was. It is surprising to me, and still is, that Dad and Mom allowed us to go out for football. It was a harsh decision then because there was so much work to do. But they did. And as it turned out, they, of course, were our biggest fans—going to every game they could. I do not remember any time that they were not there for us.

"As it turned out, both of us did well in sports—particularly football and boxing. These became our opportunities to go on with our education. Both of us played football on grant-in-aid scholarships: I at Northwestern University, Evanston, Illinois, and Connie at the University of Washington in Seattle, Washington.

"Connie was a leader with his peers and in his activities with others. He would work hard to get things done faster so he could go and have time with his friends. There were some chores that we had to do, and Connie would have his friends in to help get chores done faster so he could go and do what he had his mind set on to do."

Strong Mind, Strong Body

It was during this wonderful time of life—the school years—that Connie's strong body and natural love of and ability at sports became very apparent. Spurred on by older brother Don's great ability at most sports, Connie would become a standout over these years in football, boxing, speed skating, hockey, baseball, and— well, just about anything he tried.

Bill cites a favorite story: "Poverty would be a word that could describe most of our years as a family. It was serious poverty. Yet, with that reality, we never were wanting for medical attention or food. When Connie was 14 or 15, he came to my dad and asked for fifty cents to get his racer skates welded for an ice race. Dad felt badly, but he said he just didn't have the money. Connie understood. The next day, Connie came home carrying the first-place trophy. He had beaten all challengers. He had wired the skates together to make them hold for the races. When he presented the trophy to our father, Dad cried. He was so touched and hurt that he hadn't had the money Connie needed."

Bill hadn't remembered the part of the story, however, that this was a competition that had been advertised over several towns and counties in northern Illinois. To get to the lake being used for the competition, Connie and a few cronies had to walk five miles each way just to get there and back.

"Connie was always very competitive," Bill states. "Whether he was boxing or playing marbles, he played to win."

The importance of the closeness of the family shines through in another story Bill recalls.

"When I was quite young, I contracted scarlet fever. I was quarantined at home with my mother and father. Don and Connie stayed at the home of a friend. They would walk home and talk to us through a window. After a couple of days, Connie announced that he was sick. Dad, thinking he might be coming down with the fever, asked him to come in. When Connie stepped into the house, he broke into a great big smile. Dad said, 'I thought you were sick.' Connie said, 'I am—*homesick.*' In he stayed for the duration.

"I remember a time that Connie was driving our dad's newly purchased very old car," Bill continued. "The tie-rod fell off and Connie could not steer the car. I was a young passenger. We went down an embankment, and it became obvious that we were going to hit a telephone pole at a fairly good speed. Connie threw himself between the dash and me. We broke the pole in two, but because of Connie's action, I was unhurt."

Almost as an afterthought, and yet too important not to mention, Bill adds, "I remember Connie struggling with the issue of the ministry. I saw him actually sit and sob in confusion. He was heavily torn between the ministry and coaching and teaching. This was a profound struggle for him most of one summer.

"To say that my brothers have influenced my life would be an understatement. They have had a profound influence. We were raised with a sense of pride. Out of that family of limited means and unlimited dreams came a total of over 28 years of post high school education. It evolved two excellent clergymen and one moderately good district judge; not bad for one mom and dad." (*JWW note:* No, Bill not bad at all. You see, under this family's influence, "The Light Goes On.")

School Days, Good Old Golden Rule Days . . .

Of equal importance to the family influence during this era was the schooling experience.

Connie attended first grade in northern Illinois. Sure enough, the work situation required the family to relocate back to Herrick during Connie's second and third grades. It was during that third year that Connie experienced the illness mentioned earlier and would require a repeat of the third grade. This marked a period of rapid and pronounced development for Connie to the point that almost sixty years later Connie sees the repeat of the third grade as a true blessing.

First, it was back to northern Illinois and enrolling in Big Hollow Elementary School. This was a one-room schoolhouse with all eight grades present. It was also Connie's first meeting with Mrs. Rich. Many of us have that one teacher in our background who surely must have been sent from a special place in heaven for the express purpose of lighting our fire for education. For Conrad Walker, that was Mrs. Rich.

Connie was already a good reader, thanks to the example and encouragement of Grandma Cindy and Bebe, his dear sainted mother, as well as his dad's love for the history of this beloved country. Now Connie became aware of the reasons that reading was so very important, how the total of the life's experiences were enriched through reading.

The hidden blessing of having to repeat the third grade began to manifest itself in very tangible ways at this time. Since the very earliest days, the Walker boys were subjected to a most hearty way of life. The legacy of their dad, Don Dougal: stringent work ethic, hard body, sound mind, and self-sufficiency were apparent to all. The fact that now Connie was a bit older than his classmates, coupled with athletic ability and natural outgoing personality, did not go unnoticed by Mrs. Rich. She used the older students to assist the younger students and helped develop leaders and readers.

About this particular time, Connie said, "'Twas a great delight—a most meaningful moment in time under Mrs. Rich. She was a truly caring and inspiring person in my life as a youngster."

Indeed, the seeds of leadership, mentoring, and teaching were being sown.

It was a time of blending strong family values with the discoveries and the developing of all that early formal education had to offer. Every day at school would become an adventure for this young, eager, and talented observer of all that life had to offer.

Connie's days would be filled with learning, while evenings, weekends, and summers were spent doing chores: wood cutting, hunting and trapping—always a garden—and the job of all jobs, the cement gang. Connie and brother Don were paid men's wages by their dad, but they truly earned it. They had to buy all their own clothes, entertainment etc. The first year or so, Connie was the sandpile man. Then, on to the rock pile, until, finally, both Connie and Don were mixers and haulers and full-fledged equals to any rock-hard contractors around.

Connie would also tend to younger brother Bill, who accompanied him on treks to the traps that he had set, harvesting muskrat, mink, fox, beavers and so on. Often, Connie would (during the winter months) skate for miles up the lakes and rivers checking traps and visiting with friends. All of these activities were developing an extraordinarily robust and well-conditioned athlete.

It's worthy of mention that at the fifth-grade level Connie moved into a more conventional school, Gavin Elementary. While at Gavin, Connie would be reunited with Mrs. Rich as a teacher and mentor. Connie will ever be grateful and blessed by this re-connection. What a dear and caring influence this marvelous lady was for so many students and this young Walker boy in particular.

On to Grant High School

Four defining years were spent at Grant High School. There was so much to do, so little time.

Connie was the class president three of four years at Grant, which may give some indication of the impact this young Viking would have on those around him for all the years of his life. He was so effective that, half a century later, each former classmate this writer contacted and those who attended the 50th class reunion (held while this record was being written) still looked upon this blessed man as the leader of the group.

In an effort to not over-dramatize the impact that Connie had on his classmates at Grant High, and yet convey some of the true emotion he engendered, perhaps the words of a former classmate, Donna (Follensbee) Harrison, now of Surprise, Arizona, following the reunion might do the trick.

I did not travel in the same group as Connie in high school, but it being a rather small school I knew him well and considered him a friend. His qualities are so tremendous and he is revered by so many. Our friendship was renewed through planning and implementing our half-century class reunion. Oh, what a bonus in life...a truly wonderful weekend.

One thing that stands out in my mind about the night of our reunion banquet is that he and I were co-masters-of-ceremonies for the program. I had asked a mate, unbeknownst to Connie, to give a special blessing to Connie, directing the participation of all. I just knew that Connie would be *so* surprised, and he was. Midway through the program I simply announced that we had something not on the program to do, and I called upon this particular mate to come up to the microphone.

I don't know if this mate had a little too much to drink, was nervous, or what it might have been, but he opened his presentation with a joke. As he began, I wondered where he was going with it and why. It was rather out of place since I implied that he would be doing something regarding Connie when I introduced him. Well, the story was a bit off-color. You could hear a pin drop, and then you heard this big deep Santa Claus laugh as only Connie can do, and of course the rest of the audience joined in, the presenter smiled, and proceeded with a very nice prayer. What a great guy is Connie; he came through and saved everyone from deep embarrassment.

Later that evening Connie and I worked together bringing laughter and tears to our mates. I remembered 50 years ago sitting next to Connie awaiting our turns to approach the microphone at our graduation. We were the speakers at our commencement exercises. Connie was to be the featured speaker. We were so honored to speak that night under the stars out on the football field facing our parents and friends. Sitting next to Connie that night helped to calm my nerves and shaking knees, and standing next to him 50 years later had the same effect. What a guy!

Thanks for thinking of me. I am so very honored to be considered a friend of Conrad N. Walker. I must say again, what a guy!

One anecdote in particular, which might point up the degree of importance of Connie's personal stature and omnipresence to his classmates, has been preserved.

Remembering that in the '40s and '50s hazing was not only prevalent in most schools and fraternities, it was often quite inappropriate and frequently even physically harmful.

Connie, an imposing and forthright person even at this young and tender age, went through all that the hazers had to offer, but he made it abundantly clear that the student body must "relax to the point of control." In other words, do what you feel you must and is appropriate, but do not bring harm to, in Connie's words, "my classmates." The student body wisely demurred.

Connie readily admits that, while he was never the possessor of the highest grade-point average in class, he was generally in the upper standings. Even to this day, Connie feels that the interest and continual involvement with reading is the basis for any academic achievement that he has encountered during this era and all years to follow. He gives daily thanks to his Grandma Cindy, his dad and mom, and the marvelous Mrs. Rich for this lifelong interest.

In retrospect, it is apparent to one observing Connie's high school years that academics were a significant factor in defining what was to be the Connie Walker from there forward. In his senior yearbook, for example, his life desire was listed as either a teacher and coach or a minister.

It further seems extreme that he was able to maintain a high academic standing, considering his extra involvements, which amazingly never became distractions. School athletics, many spiritually-oriented activities, which we will take a much closer look at shortly, and an attractive young lady or two (one in particular), were a big part of Connie's world during these years.

That wasn't all, however. The following laundry list may give some insight to the kind of enthusiastic approach to life this young stalwart would display all of his years: played the sousaphone all four years of high school; sang in the school choir and glee club (some say vigorously) all four years; was constantly involved with student politics; would take on a mentoring project at the drop-of-a-hat; was very involved with church activities; and he displayed extraordinary entrepreneurial tendencies.

Besides the already-mentioned chores of wood cutting, gardening, hunting, etc., there were the paid employments: cement crew, alternating with his brother Don and with assistance from his brother Bill, working at Bebe's Hamburger Café (a ten stool café that Bebe had for several years), the lawn-mowing service that grew to the point that he had to hire friends to help, and the garbage collection business he started along with his dad and brother Don.

Let's Talk Sports

Years before, Don Dougal had told both Don and Connie that they could not count on college unless they qualified for grant-in-aid assistance. He then made sure the boys were men of integrity, had strong, hard bodies, and a will to win. He and Bebe then supported them in all their activities, and the rest was up to them. It was enough.

Connie has always felt that brother Don's athletic prowess opened doors for Connie in high school. By the time Connie got to Grant High as a freshman, Don was a senior and well established as one tough jock. Connie says simply that Don was the best of the best.

All that may be so; however, it remains true that Connie made the varsity football team as a freshman. That was almost unheard of in those days. Connie says he made it as a kicker, punter, and extra point man because of his educated toe. He also played a lot of guard—both ways.

As brother Don relates, "In high school, boxing was a varsity sport in those days. In the ring we knew and respected each other. Dad did not want us to compete against each other. I believe that he discouraged the coach from ever putting us in the ring together. I was old enough to be the senior and heavyweight of our team. I have no doubt, had Connie been the same age, my place on the team would have been in jeopardy, for I had never known Connie not to be a fearless and competitive scrapper. He became an excellent athlete competing in both boxing and football."

Brother Bill's earlier remark, "Connie was always very competitive, whether boxing or playing marbles, he played to win," somehow now had more meaning.

Another voice from the past is heard from Edwin Rostad, classmate, now of Grayslake, Illinois.

Connie and I go back a long way to Grant High School days. We were boxing buddies, sport buddies, and classmates. He was always ambitious and focused on the matter at hand. He helped me with boxing and football and sports in general. Connie was a caring and sharing person.

Connie Walker is a deeply religious and patriotic person, and I wish him many more years of greatness and life.

Here is another response, from Frank (Duke) Watts, classmate (now of Winter Park, Colorado).

My primary contact with Connie in high school was definitely sports centered. And those days were a treasure. The big war was over and the

Korean War was heating up but was still only a distant possibility for us. Most of us were too busy just growing up. We had left the swimming holes of our youth to discover high school and its glory in real organized sports, girls, and new friends. That is where I met Connie Walker.

He was a quiet, gentle, big guy. He seemed to protect us little guys by his mere presence. I came to know Connie as a fierce competitor in football, boxing, baseball, basketball, track and hockey. He seemed to be a man among boys.

He played both ways in football, and when we needed yardage, we ran behind Connie. When we needed a big play on defense, it seemed that Connie was always there. I recall one play in particular where Connie led a sweep around right end and knocked two opponents on their "duffs" for a crucial long gainer. Grant was a small school, but we did some great deeds.

Connie was our catcher on the baseball team and the clean-up hitter (what else?). I remember that he was the discus and shot-put man on the track team and took home many conference firsts.

I think that Connie had taken up boxing before he came to Grant. With an outstanding athlete for an older brother, it was probably in self-defense. Connie was our heavyweight, and I don't ever remember him losing a fight. He had a snap to his punches that put many an opponent on the canvas.

He was involved with every activity that presented itself: band, choir, school politics and more. But he always remained in the top 10 percent of our class. He was driven to God, even then. Our yearbook indicates his ambition to be a minister or a teacher. My knowledge of his life since high school tells me that he has been both, as well as an outstanding college athlete, a husband, father, grandfather and a true American hero.

The telling thing about these and other accounts (too numerous to record here) is how vivid and heartfelt they are remembered—over fifty years after the fact!

God Becomes a *Major* Player

The third influence on the development of the Conrad N. Walker that the world knows today was the spiritual aspect.

It has been noted several times that Grandma Cindy, mother Bebe, and other family members had a tremendous impact on Connie's earliest years. However, there was one person, a true man of God who came upon the scene, one who was to be huge in Connie's development.

Brother Don remembers, "Faith came into the picture early on. I know that there was no church in our town until I was nine years old, and Connie was near eight. But this was early enough for me to see that church, spirituality, and God had an early effect on his life. He loved our pastors. Later, when it came time for confirmation instruction, he especially loved and respected the one who trained him: Pastor Owen Gangstead. There is no doubt in my mind where the convincing took place in his life that Christ was real and a living personal Lord!"

The following remembrance comes from this most cherished person, Pastor Owen Gangstead, resident of Decorah, Iowa, who at the time of this writing was a bit over ninety years and a bit less than one hundred. He has since gone to his promised rest with the Lord Jesus.

On a cold January morning, I met a young teenager by the name of Connie (sometimes called Norman) Walker. That Saturday gathering of early teeners was the confirmation class. Each Saturday for two years, this group met with the pastor of Trinity Lutheran Church. Assignments were from the Bible, the Catechism, church history, and was a time for giving and sharing in events in their lives.

In due time, the young folks in that class finished their two-year period of instruction. In a very meaningful worship service, they publicly declared their faith in the arisen God. Connie was in that group. I noted that he had something different about him. For instance, he came to me one day and asked me if he could take another year. A third year of classes! That has never happened—before or since—and I have been teaching a very long time.

Our young people also saw something different in Connie, and they elected him as the president of Luther League. At this time, plans were in the making for a youth gathering of 8,000 teenagers. It was to be held in Saskatoon, Canada. All of our teens worked to build up the treasury so they could help Connie represent them at the convention.

One huge project was collecting newspapers. Don Walker (Connie's dad) had a garbage route. He made his big truck available for the collecting of newspapers. One Sunday, we were gathered at the church with Connie. His truck was full to overflowing. He took it to the collecting agency in

Waukegan, Illinois. It brought a goodly chunk of money. Connie would be able to go with a large part of his expenses covered.

Connie was an excellent athlete, nearing two hundred pounds. One Saturday he brought several of his teammates to the church. A very tough opponent stood in the way of a championship. About 10:00 A.M. Connie and his teammates gathered around the altar in a special prayer service. Who do you suppose won the game? You're right—Connie and his prayer supporters.

After high school, Connie was awarded a scholarship to play football at the University of Washington. I took him to a place northwest of Chicago. There he joined another recruit for the U. of W. It was with a heavy heart that I bid him farewell, for I feared that the years ahead might be destructive to his Christian Faith. Praise God, word came back to me that he was leading the football team in Bible study!

Since Connie was ordained in 1959, his has been a rich ministry. Only in eternity will we ever know the huge number who are or will be in Heaven because Connie Walker pointed them in the direction that they must take. (*JWW note:* Pastor Gangstead asked me, "Sir, does this help?" My reply was, "Pastor, you'll never know how much. God Bless.")

Connie remembers the "right man at the right time" saying, "One of the greatest gifts of God was a pastor who came to our village of Long Lake, Illinois, at just the proper time for the Walker family. Yes, many great pastors came before and after Owen Gangstead, but he was a special agent of God for us. He came to the people, and he called and gave hope and meaning in the Lord wherever he went.

"In our confirmation instruction, he made our classes come alive—they were vibrant and indeed challenging and captivating. He was a true shepherd, a deeply spiritual man of prayer and teaching. The Christian life took on a whole fresh, new and deeper meaning. The assurance of salvation became clear and full of verve, vigor and life. The Holy Spirit used this faithful pastor and servant of God every day of his life, even as a *senior*, senior citizen, and he spent several hours each day in prayer.

"This devout encourager/pastor stimulated a special closeness with Father and Mother, my brothers and myself. He, in a most exciting portrayal of pastoring, shepherding, and mentoring, was used by God to have us pray about the holy ministry. The whole drama of ministry was held before us—with our strengths *and* our weaknesses. The strengths were first amplified and then the weaknesses and sins of thought, word, and deed.

"The Holy Spirit used this special agent/ambassador to put joy and jubilance back into the faith life. Law was first utilized to convict of sin, and the sweet sure ring of the Gospel personally sounded forth, and seared into our persons—in our hearts—in our very being." Praise God!

The light having come on during this era through family values, education and spiritually, perhaps it's time to go to college, but first . . .

CHAPTER-UNNUMBERED

THIS IS TOO IMPORTANT
FOR A NUMBER

Genesis 2:18. "Then the Lord said, it is not good for
the man to be alone; I will provide a partner for him."-
NEB

Some happenings that took place during the high
school years were just too important to include with
everything else!

As Connie was beginning his sophomore year at
Grant High, he became aware of two very impressive
things. First, it seemed to him that those students who
handed in neatly typed assignments received about one
full grade point over those who didn't. Secondly, he
noticed a senior who was the fastest typist, not only in
school, but quite possibly the fastest in the state.

Oh! I almost forgot to mention that Joan "Ann"
Wicinski was as attractive as anyone Connie had ever
seen before—or since.

It was at this time that Mr. Orr (Connie's boxing
coach) decided to take the boxing team to Chicago for
the Golden Gloves matches (a well-deserved incentive
and thank you trip). The first inkling Ann had that

Connie was interested in her was when he asked her to go with him to watch the matches. Connie can't remember a great deal about the matches, but fifty-plus years later, he remembers the bus trip to Chicago. In Connie's words, "We sat in the back of the bus, occasionally rubbing noses—and that hasn't stopped yet."

Years later, when asked about her reaction to Connie's interest, Ann (who stands five feet even) stated, "Well, I was astonished. We were in different 'clicks.' I was—well—*me*, and he was this big, popular jock."

The noble Owen Gangstead, pastor, very gladly offered this:

Let me introduce you to a renowned and faithful person in the life of Connie Walker. Her name is Ann.

Ann and Connie will tell you how she was both mother and father when he was far away from home in Vietnam and other places.

I would share with you an incident from their courtship days. These two dear folks decided to live as life partners in holy matrimony. Ann had been raised in a Christian community—her home, albeit a different communion. They decided that it was imperative that they be of one mind and spirit. Ann, therefore, made the decision to join Connie as a Lutheran. (*JWW note:* Not an easy or popular decision in a very traditional Polish Catholic family.).

Knowing Ann, we can be sure that the decision was the correct one. What a helpmate! What a mother! What a friend! To prepare for membership in the Lutheran church, she walked several miles each week to study with me the basic doctrine of Scripture and the Lutheran church. God bless precious Ann.

As the eldest child, Ann was expected to work at a full-time job and bring home the paycheck to help make ends meet until age 21. This she did, faithfully. Being Ann, however, in her resourcefulness, she also maintained a second and sometimes a third job to prepare for those predictably difficult first years of the impending union, which would ultimately come after a five-year courtship.

(*JWW note:* With this very important business finished, let's go to the University of Washington. From here on, we hear a lot from Connie in his own words.)

YOUNG LOVE—TRUE LOVE

A QUARTERBACK'S WORST NIGHTMARE

CHAPTER 4

THE UNIVERSITY OF WASHINGTON

Psalm 119:73. "Thy hands molded me and made me what I am; show me how I may learn thy commandments."-NEB

Acts 1:8. "But you will receive power when the Holy Spirit comes upon you; and you will bear witness for me . . . to the ends of the earth."-NEB

My deep desire was to attend one of the fine church universities, and I was in serious correspondence with several. At that time, however, they could only render minimum assistance for athletic grant-in-aid or scholarships.

Our family needs were such that I had to attend where there was considerable assistance in the realm of grant-in-aid programs. My beloved elder brother, Don, had already paved the way for interest and attention in me by Big Ten schools. Don was a standout as a most noteworthy lineman for Northwestern University's stellar football team. He was a great athlete in both football and boxing and could have easily moved into the pro-ranks, particularly with the Chicago Bears.

The Walker family is a family of patriots. At that historic time in history, our nation (along with others) was in combat with North Korea and later Red China. Brother Don, as mentioned earlier, came on active duty with the U.S. Navy after graduation from Northwestern University with multiple degrees.

It was brother Don's athletic prowess and his own mighty high school accomplishments that caused real interest in me by several Big Ten schools, as well as the Southland conference (primarily Tulane) and the West Coast.

Two boosters, Mr. Joe Dubsky and Dr. Alfred Strauss from the University of Washington, contacted and visited me in a most convincing manner on behalf of the University of Washington.

After a long and prayerful decision-making process, I selected the University of Washington, a most prestigious academic university and an upper division West Coast football team. The U. of W. Huskies football team was a vigorous, challenging, demanding, and growing adventure. It was a magnificent training ground for a person to prepare for the life-changing and exacting call to be a pastor, a shepherd of our Lord's flock.

Football with the Huskies, under coaches Howie O'Dell and Johnny Cherberg, was exciting and packed with friendships, fun and most of all *very* hard work. I earned my keep as a hard-working and motivated lineman for the U. of W. but did not fully excel, as I remained a reserve lineman. I played enough, however, to interest and attract several pro teams (including the St. Louis Cardinals, the 49'ers and the Green Bay Packers) all asking me for a tryout.

The prospect was enticing, but the time line was in conflict with the opening of classes at Luther Seminary, St. Paul, Minnesota—and I blessedly and clearly knew that I was called to be a pastor. Within our family tradition and teachings, when you are called, you are called by the Holy Spirit, and you keep your hand on the plow until you finish the course to be a shepherd/ pastor.

During the football off-season, I continued with training and participation in the boxing world. Boxing is a most wonderful character-building sport and a sport of mighty physical conditioning. The object is to hit and not *get* hit. It teaches fast-moving discipline and quick decision making. I held Midwest and West Coast heavyweight titles during those formative years (being a boxer definitely increases your capacity to suffer).

Boxing proved to be a most helpful and valuable tool for, and the execution of, the role of pastor/chaplain over the years; I actively coached boxing during my entire Army career. Whether I was dressed in the vestments of the altar or the trunks of the ring, many soldiers came to the Lord during our coaching of boxing and our caring and friendly relationships. Many friendships were formed both in the gym and out on the daily seven-mile run.

The door to the boxing pro-ranks was grandly opened before me with some lavish offers. Again, however, I knew that by the grace of God I had a clear call of the Lord to prepare to be a servant-shepherd-pastor. We kept our hand on the plow and maintained single-mindedness toward the holy ministry. I praise God for the blessing of boxing!

Frat Boy

As a U. of W. student and an athlete, I became a member of the Sigma Nu Fraternity. The members proved to be lasting friends and truly vibrant, winsome persons and leaders. They were mentors in the area of fine study habits and social skills. A big plus developed when each Monday evening after the chapter meeting, and for several years, we had a well-attended Bible study. (*JWW note:* Connie initiated this study.)

For a period of time we were laughed at on campus, but the laughter moved to respect and a degree of admiration, and other Bible studies began to flourish.

Connie as a "Knight in Shining Armor"—Sort of!

At the Sigma Nu house, I had a helpful sponsor who assisted with room and board. This kind person died, leaving me in dire need.

A neighboring sorority needed a head houseboy to supervise and work in the kitchen, clean up, and serve the young women at their tables. New friends were made, but there was a hard and fast rule: "No dating of the young women in the sorority or the consequence is immediate firing!"

As the head houseboy, I always had to have a couple of young men ready for employment at a moment's notice. I indeed had a rapid turnover of personnel since a worker would come in and work for a short time— until he found a friend and yes, he would be fired.

At this time, panty raids were the craze. The idea was to break into sorority houses and women's dorms and steal panties (usually from dresser drawers) and display them as trophies.

A late evening phone call from the house mother produced a frantic, "Connie, come quickly, we need your help!" I rushed over to the sorority house and not a moment too soon. Dozens of young men came charging down the sidewalk leading to the front door where I stood as sentinel. Fortunately, one of the raider leaders was a fellow Washington Huskie lineman. I said, "Friend, take them next door," and he did, bless him!

Most of our dear young women were elated not to suffer having their undergarments on display as trophies on the campus. A few of the sorority women seemed to be angry at me, however, as they desired to have that adventure well placed in their memory books.

There was, however, a lot of "Right Thinking"

Next door to the fraternity house was the Luther House, the meeting area and spiritual growth place for Lutheran Christians, both the student body and faculty. All inquirers and searchers were welcomed with joy and open arms.

I will be ever grateful for the Christian leadership of Bonnie Sorem, Pastor Al Dillemuth, and Ruth Klingsmith during those vital and formative years at the U. of W. A person of great importance to me at the university was Pastor Ed Hummond, one of the most caring teacher/pastors I've known.

During those grand days at the U. of W., other meaningful and spiritually deepening opportunities took place. A fellow athlete and friend, Jerry Kirk (who became one of the notables in the Presbyterian church as a pastor/proclaimer), a true master, introduced me to the exciting and rigorous Bible memorization programs of the Navigators.

The Navigators are magnificent teachers of the Word of God and very fine trainers in personal discipleship and the disciplining of young Christians. Thanks be to God! I was raised in a church fellowship that clearly taught the Word and memorization of the Word of our Lord and the deep prayer life. The Navigator folks became real encouragers with their organized study, memorization, and application-enhancement program.

At about the same time, two dear Presbyterian brothers, Jerry Kirk and Dick Simmons, invited me as a U. of W. athlete to participate with them in the high schools' "Young Life" outreach and personal witness to our Lord Jesus. Jerry and Dick are fine models today for youth fellowships all over the military and civilian church parishes, and to this very hour they are disciplining, witnessing, and caring for young people in the Kingdom of God.

My cup of blessings continued to run over. I had the goodness and steadfast love of the Lord and relational and caring friends who assisted in my Christian growth. The deepening will and grace of God was very apparent as leading after leading to place after place underlined the call to be a shepherd and pastor of our Lord's flock.

It was through the Lutheran Student Fellowship that I was seriously introduced to spiritual retreats and great Bible study groups. It was here that I found life-enriching fellowship with truly fun-loving and humorous God-loving Christian people. It was a time of boundless joy to remember the wonderful experience of the retreats and day-to-day fellowships, sippin' and lippin', then and to this day.

During those years as a Washington Huskie, I also went out on deputation teams to speak in the community and the extended community on the importance of studies, athletics, leadership, sportsmanship, and the faith life.

Of Special Importance

My cherished and precious high school sweetheart, Joan (Ann) Wicinski, came to Seattle after she was twenty-one and stayed with the Wistrand family for a year. Ann secured a great job in Seattle with the D. K. McDonald Insurance Company and did exceedingly well because of her tremendous skills as secretary and typist. Ann has excelled all of her working life.

We were wed on the 16th day of December 1953 at the University Lutheran Church with Pastors Al Dillamuth and Ed Hummond officiating. What a most blessed and phenomenal union and oneness in Christ this marriage has been for over half a century. We had courted for over five years before marriage. Spontaneous? Perhaps not!

Our loved daughter Beverly Ann was conceived in Seattle and born after graduation from the U. of W., the 7th of February 1955 in Libertyville, Illinois. God is so good!

An exclamation mark must be thankfully acknowledged. Letters, letters! There were letters of care, love, inspiration, and encouragement from precious family and friends, and beloved Pastor Owen Gangstead, and even members of my home church. These were so very important and so very influential; knowing that they surrounded us all in prayer in our Lord's name. On a personal level, I believe that this is important: all of our informational e-mail helpers are of keen assistance; however, a *personal* handwritten (or printed) letter is a relational communication piece that is of immense value and is most significant.

In December 1954, we were packed and ready to leave Seattle even though the university still owed me two quarters of grant-in-aid I had an assignment as youth director at my home parish, Long Lake, Illinois, and a fantastic opportunity to work with a precious pastor, Myron Hoff.

As I went to say farewell to my university advisor and pick up my degree in sheepskin, I was understandably concerned when he came out of his office with a rather ashen look and said, "I'm sorry, Connie, I figured incorrectly. I cannot give you your degree; you need five more credits." Believe me, this was no way to start a fun-filled day.

Not wishing to dwell on negative and painful memories, let me say that I quickly (and prayerfully) registered for five hours of academic wonderment, consisting of two hours of English Literature and three hours of the Philosophy of Aesthetics. These courses were painfully completed during our months as youth director at Trinity Lutheran in Illinois. The University of Washington then sent along my degree.

On to Seminary

In late August 1955, we were off in our old Chevrolet from Long Lake, Illinois to St. Paul, Minnesota, and Luther Seminary.

I was in an attitude of thanksgiving and awe the first adventurous time that I walked onto the campus of Luther Seminary in St. Paul.

Luther Seminary is a beautiful and well-placed facility with considerable acreage in the city near the border between St. Paul and Minneapolis. It is an unforgettable witness, as it boldly stands.

Both the student body and the faculty captivated me—yes, saints and sinners alike filled me with awe and made me ready to go to work. It took many years of living and a storehouse of experiences before we arrived, but joy! We did arrive, and I started preparing to be a shepherd, indeed a pastor of God's people.

My beloved Ann, Beverly, and I began by seeking out housing. At that time, the seminary was not physically prepared for married students. Unable to find anything situated close to the seminary, Ann and I went to our knees asking the Lord for help. We applied for and were accepted for government housing a considerable distance from the seminary and on the third floor. We slept on the floor since we had no furniture and lived in a camping-out atmosphere for a couple of weeks.

Before we attempted to buy a few items of furniture, I told Ann that I would check the community bulletin board one more time. We had prayed, and it was there! A clear message, "Apartment for rent, corner of Como and Carter," two blocks from the seminary. I stood weeping at that corner. I called Ann. She advised, "Take it," and we did.

Wow! We realized that a home so close to the seminary would save on driving and other expenses. That evening we were on our knees praising God for all of His leading and blessings. Later on, a special delight and gift would manifest itself. Each evening as I walked home from the seminary and looked up at our window, precious daughter Beverly would be waving at her old dad. About one year later, she started lifting her younger blond sister, Miriam, to the window so both could wave at me. To this day I hold dear that sight.

Our spirits were further buoyed by the fact that we had, through much careful planning, been able to save the princely sum of $703.90 to aid us during the first year of seminary. Our third floor apartment in government housing, however, had the downside of requiring a lot of up and down staircase climbing. Ann was again with child, and she had a miscarriage shortly after we moved into our new place. We did not yet have insurance. She was hospitalized and well cared for, and her new and caring doctor and hospital bill came to (you guessed it) exactly $700.

Although we were as broke as broke could be, God was ever faithful. Other doors began to immediately open for us. I was hired as the janitor and coal furnace tender for the amount of our rent. Next, the janitorial work for a dental office in the complex opened up, and I gleefully took the job. Shortly thereafter, I was asked if I would become the custodian and caretaker at an entire nearby insurance complex building. Indeed I would! It was obvious, however, that I would need help, so I hired a fellow seminarian to assist for four hours each day.

As doors opened, we walked through with a thankful and jubilant spirit. We kept these custodial jobs during our entire four years at seminary.

We were asked to do weekend pulpit supply in the surrounding territory, which gave us a scrumptious country Sunday dinner each week and an honorarium for the worship service. This, too, continued throughout the seminary years.

We met so many beautiful persons and families in the pulpit supply churches. They were ever so kind to us, and they gave helpful and honest feedback on the sermons and proclamations of God's saving Word. These spiritual, wise, deep, and prayerful people were a delight and an inspiration as we served them and related to them in an authentic and faithful way. Bless them *all*, as they opened ministry and growth opportunities to us.

The new seminary president (1955) was Dr. Alvin Rogness. He set the tone and the kind, scholarly, evangelical and Christ-centered spirit for students and faculty alike. The faculty, to me, was the very best. All were absolute giants in the fields of teaching Biblical theology (Old and New Testaments), missionology, homiletics (art of preaching) and related areas. They were unmatched in the training of young men to be pastors and the teaching of the Word in and for the world.

We had daily chapel. We sang both great historic and gospel hymns helped by a majestic organ, which assisted the worship in a powerful and dynamic way.

Seminary friends were many, to include Irv and Marian Njus. We started seminary together and then served congregations as pastors and then on loan to the military as chaplains. We served decades together in the U.S. Army. We met annually at training missions and even retired to the same location in San Antonio, Texas. Irv and Marian are boldly faithful and prayer filled to our Lord as a ministry team, serving to this very hour.

Our class overflowed with tremendous and gifted Biblical scholars—real people—people with an extraordinary message. They were (and are) profoundly loving shepherds!

Another cherished friendship was Stanley G. West. (Stan has since become a world class writer). Since we were seated alphabetically, he not only was a seatmate but also became a dear brother in the Lord. We made adventurous plans together each autumn and went pheasant, duck, and geese hunting. Such times were times of joy and deepening trust and friendship. It also put food on the table!

One of our cherished seminary professors, Dr. Herman Preus, always alert and watchful, knew that Stan and I were often out hunting. There were times when he looked at us with a bit of scorn, asking, "Were you successful on the hunt?" Fortunately, we usually were. Our fourth year, he opened up with, "Stan and Connie, I always enjoyed you in my class, but, blast it!

Why didn't you take me along hunting?" We felt bad and had we been there for a fifth year, he would have been invited.

I can but thank and praise God for the hard-working, scholarly, spirit and grace-filled teaching, as well as the abounding friendships during those marvelous years at Luther Seminary in St. Paul, Minnesota.

Ordination was celebrated on 5 April 1959 in my home church of Trinity Lutheran in Long Lake, Illinois. The District President for Southern Minnesota, Dr. E. Rhinertson, was the ordaining shepherd/pastor along with dear pastor friends, Al Langough, "Shorty" Hjortland, and Myron Hoff, and also my special pastor/mentor and friend, Owen Gangstead. My dear and faithful brothers, Don and Bill, were the Scripture readers.

The laying on of hands and the putting on of the "stole" (the yoke of Christ Jesus) were monumentally important and meaningful moments. We were prayer and grace filled as we came to our first call as pastor and family at Shiloh Lutheran, Elmore, Minnesota.

CHAPTER 5

A TIME FOR NEW BEGINNINGS

Matthew 18:20. "For where two or three have met together in my name, I am there among them."-NEB

Matthew 28:19. "Go forth therefore, and make all nations my disciples; baptize men everywhere in the name of the Father and the Son and the Holy Spirit, and teach them . . . I am with you always to the end of time."-NEB

Early during the same period as Connie's first call to Shiloh Lutheran, he joined the Minnesota National Guard as a chaplain in the Viking Division. Connie relates, "My first beloved commander in the Battle Group Headquarters in Mankato, Minnesota, was Colonel Paul Meyer. He was a great commander, friend, and mentor and remains the same to this very hour."

Forty-three years later, Paul V. Meyer, Major General (AUSA) Retired, wrote these words to me in regard to Connie:
My close association with Connie was brief, but it left an indelible mark on my life.

It started as I was commander of a National Guard Battle Group in the Mankato area. We were assigned a young first lieutenant as our group chaplain. His home was in southern Minnesota, so it was a natural fit for him and for the units in the group. His background was just made for his assignment as chaplain: young, dedicated to his religion; he was athletic and had a deep concern for those young soldiers in the various companies.

He made an impression on all during the first training camp at Camp Ripley. With his athletic background, he organized a sports program and especially a boxing program. The men in the units had someone who was interested in their morale and their religious well being. He held services in the field and visited all the units to see if there was a need for his help.

Shortly after our return from field training, he approached me and asked if I would approve his application for full-time duty with the Army as a chaplain. I said I would gladly do it, although we would miss his services. In visiting with him about his request, I asked him, "What service do you want to be in?" and his answer was, "Airborne Infantry." My next question was, "Why that?" to which he replied, "I want to be where the danger is the greatest and the need for personal counseling and prayer would be needed and helpful."

He was sent to Vietnam early in that war's history. Between assignments, he came to Mankato and visited me, and I asked him if he would speak to our local Kiwanis Club.

His remarks were emotional as he talked about holding dying soldiers in his arms, helping the wounded handle their aches, acting as a go-between for many of the soldiers and their families at home, etc. Through the years he has kept me informed of his activities in the ministry through annual letters. He has been a blessing to many, and I am one of those blessed to be his friend.

A star athlete, a wonderful family man, an individual dedicated to his Lord, and an individual with a deep personal concern for his fellow soldiers; truly a Soldier's Chaplain.

When not in Uniform, How about Vestment?

Many of us have had a period of time in our lives that is so dear, so remarkable, that surely it shall remain forever as memories in our hearts and in our souls, as long as life remains with us. Such a period of time was the late 1950s and early 1960s for the Walker family, especially Connie.

In Elmore, Minnesota, Connie found, through the grace of God, the perfect catalyst allowing Connie to make the awesome transition from a young athlete and scholar (with all the potential a person could hope for), and the underpinnings of a legend in God's Kingdom— to that marvelous, wonderful attainment—pastor/shepherd.

(*JWW note*: For the following lengthy narrative, I'm going to stay out of Connie's way, as more and more will be Connie's direct writing.)

Shiloh Days

Shiloh Lutheran was a most exciting place to be for our first call. The parishioners were deep and mature, spiritual, and Christ-centered people. They dearly and markedly enhanced our lives of study in the Word and prayer.

Most notable in our hand-in-hand walk together was the grand use of the hymns of the church, for devotions and praying resources packed with power in the Holy Spirit. It was and is truly a congregation of vigorously singing people.

A prime example was Deacon Emeritus Matt Teigland. At that time, he had recently moved in from the farm in retirement. During this era, Deacon Matt was in his late 70s and early 80s. The neighbors said that Matt always got more milk than most of his neighbors because he always sang to his cows—in both Norwegian and English.

During all five years at Shiloh Lutheran, I never once saw Deacon Matt open a hymnal. It seemed that all the hymns were written on the table of his heart, and he sang out boldly with his beautifully clear tenor voice—even as a senior/senior citizen.

Hymnology and singing was very important to the people of God at Shiloh Lutheran. They always had a broad-aged choir of youth, middle-aged, and seniors; they also had special quartets, many soloists, and duets. (Andre and Arden Torkelson and many others come to mind even after all of these years.)

Many of the youth took piano and guitar lessons and a few took instruction on the organ, led by the gifted Lorene Dray. The congregation knew that many of the youth would have to leave the Elmore area for employment. They were motivated, therefore, to prepare musical leaders for worship, wherever they went.

This was a sound, caring, and evangelical principle: to send musical, Biblical and prayer leadership young people out to the work-a-day world in many geographic locations as well as the military.

The periodic and church year concerts and dramas that were given by that very special church were a witness of the first order. The youth and the senior choirs worked as a team to present a witness, particularly during the Advent and Christmas seasons. Also of note were the efforts during the Lenten and blessed Easter celebration of prayer, praise and thanksgiving. They also prepared for certain national days of importance and remembrance, i.e., the Fourth of July, Memorial Day and special community days such as the 17th of May—Norwegian Independence Day.

It Wasn't All Music

The confirmation of youth was a particularly important time. The class worked hard, played hard, and was confronted hard if the confirmation class lessons were slighted and not given primary attention and devout care.

One dramatic day, several confirmands came in ill-equipped for the instruction in the faith class. This lack of preparedness revealed itself immediately after the opening Scripture reading and prayer by one of the confirmand classmates.

I felt that I had no choice but a sharp rebuke. I slammed the confirmation instruction book loudly in the middle of the table with a huge BANG! I then declared, "Get out of here! Do not return until you have prepared—or I will call your parents in to check out the next session!" Wow! The next week they (to the person) were super-prepared in the Word and Luther's Small Catechism.

The young people were joyous there in that special place, the instruction and study area, and ready to reveal what was written on their hearts and minds.

The youth of the parish were a cooperative, eager, and friendly group of teenagers (generally—usually—

well, most of the time). The confirmands took notes each week during the sermon. This was humbling and exciting at the same time. Most frequently, they were on target, but from time to time, some missed the mark on the message. That motivated the pastor, however, to make it clear and simple—real and alive.

One confirmation session in particular stands out in my memory. One of our precious classmates was absent from instruction. On this bright Saturday morning, I asked, "Was George present in school all week?" There was a resounding, "Yes!" This became a charming teaching moment.

The entire class walked directly to George's home and vigorously knocked on the door. George answered the door, half asleep and still in his pajamas. He invited the entire confirmation class into his home, and we proceeded to have the class. The class learned just how important each classmate was and that attendance was not to be missed unless dire family needs dictated. From that point on, attendance was near perfect, and all had a smile on their face and joy in their hearts. George to this day is a Christian and a civic leader in his community.

The young people had their own weekly prayer breakfast in the church parlors prior to school classes. They ate well and shared the Good News in an exciting and ready-to-use form. The study and prayer fellowship was at their behest. They wanted it and they made it work, using their own Biblically-oriented, creative, and sparkling minds.

The families of the parish provided adult leadership to assist the youth events and enterprises. It was a gift to work with such alive, robust, and caring people, training in leadership and purposeful and meaningful Christian lives.

(*JWW note:* Okay, Connie, I don't want to work you too hard, so I'll take it for a while.)

Adventures are Where You Find Them

Home visitations for Connie were both expected by the congregation and eagerly anticipated by the pastor. New members and visitors were first called upon by the lay leadership and then by the pastor: a truly sound evangelical principle. Since a part of the congregation lived on the Iowa side of the state line, it represented a strong commitment on the part of the church leadership and staff to visit at home or work, as necessary.

As stringent as was the home visitation schedule, the hospital visits were even more demanding. Hospital calls were generally spread over a fifty-mile radius and often required the three hundred mile round trip to the Twin Cities (Minneapolis/St. Paul). The calls were made with hymnal, the Lutheran Catechism, and God's Holy Word. Connie was invariably prepared for holy communion on his visits. These were the items that he would depend on through all of the adventures of his "storied" life.

Illustrating the fact that events surrounding those "blessed to be a blessing" can be troublesome were a couple of incidents early in Connie's Elmore years.

Yes, the congregation's spirit was strong—but, alas, the building was weak!

The very first wedding that Connie performed at Shiloh Lutheran was highlighted by an earthquake-like occurrence. Early in the service, with the young groom and lovely bride-to-be standing at the altar, the much-overused and past-its-prime flooring began to slightly give way. As everyone regained their composure (as best they could) and the immediate trauma lessened,

Connie leaned forward and whispered to the apprehensive groom, "If things break loose, you grab the altar rail and I'll take care of the bride."

On another occasion during a meeting of the young people, the church's boiler blew up like a World War II hand grenade. Praise God there were no injuries; however, nearly one hundred soot-covered young people found themselves with very thorough baths and scrubbings. Connie remembers they looked like a whole bunch of raccoons.

Not long after the Walkers arrived in Elmore, there was an incident that would bring Connie into "one" with the community, a bit beyond the normal pastor / congregation relationship.

One day, word went out of a possible drowning at the local lake. Connie rushed to the scene to offer any support that might be needed. The chief of the volunteer fire department asked, "Pastor, can you swim?" Connie was (and is) an excellent swimmer. He immediately stripped to his undergarment and dove into the somewhat formidable body of water.

Using powerful underwater thrusts and a finely-tuned boxer's expanded lung capacity, Connie was able to cross the lake rapidly and efficiently. On his return trip, he bumped into an object that upon further inspection proved to be the blessed person being searched for. After coming up for air, Connie returned to the bottom and was able to bring the lifeless, dear soul to the surface.

The word spread quickly about the accomplishment of the new Shepherd of Shiloh Lutheran. Connie was now a fixture not only as an integral part of the volunteer fire department but also of the entire community.

Another tale to be told concerning the volunteer fire department should not be lost to the years.

The phone rang in the middle of the night. "Fire, two miles out of town, Lester Coy's barn!" was all that the operator had to say to get each of the volunteers to jump into action. Connie threw on shoes (no socks), trousers (no shorts or belt), shirt, and glasses and he was off.

When he arrived, the barn was well involved. The chief came up to Connie and said "Pastor, I think we can take care of the bottom okay, but you're a big strong fella. Do you think that you can get up on top of this stack of hay bales and handle a hose by yourself to try to salvage the roof?" Without a moment's hesitation, Connie grabbed the hose and started climbing. Once on top and the water pressure was unleashed, Connie had to wrap both arms around the hose to effectively control and direct the flow.

It didn't take long for Connie to realize that a few more seconds at the parsonage putting on shorts and a belt would have been time well spent. Connie not only had to concentrate on the humanitarian task at hand, but also had to develop several new dance steps and body contortions to try to keep his beltless trousers from continuing to go south.

This became more important, remembering that in rural America, the never-fail formula for getting the whole town together was to (a) have a tent meeting; (b) have an ice cream social; or (c) have a fire.

Just as Connie had reconciled himself with the thought that pastoral dignity within the community was about to be compromised, he felt the big, powerful hands of 70-year-old Otto Lang around his waist. Otto deftly secured Connie's migrating trousers with a piece of bailing twine. Connie would long remember Otto's booming voice in the clear night air saying, "We can't have my pastor's derriere exposed to the whole community, now can we?" Otto was the coffee klatch hero for a couple of weeks thereafter.

> Proverbs 17:22. "A merry heart makes a cheerful countenance, but low spirits saps a man's strength."- NEB

For half a century of soul shepherding, the element of humor has always been of paramount importance to Connie Walker, and it is with sincere glee that the uplifting stories roll off his tongue with clarity and appreciation.

One such concerned the first (typically harsh) winter the pastor spent in Elmore.

One bright but cold, wintry weekday as Connie made his way downtown on the main street, he happened across one of his parishioner's car with the hood up and the parishioner obviously very concerned. Connie, ever the Good Samaritan, went over to console and give aid as he could. Looking at the engine, it was obvious that there was a fire.

Acting like the problem solver that he has always been, Connie grabbed a nearby snow shovel and started shoveling some of the very plentiful snow onto the distressed engine. From several hundred feet away, two of the ladies of the congregation stood witnessing their pastor feeding this stationary open-hooded auto a snow diet; and one lady was prompted to ask the other, "Do you suppose the pressure is getting to Pastor Walker?"

Once again, Connie had made the coffee klatch circuit.

Connie Gets into the Cattle Business (Sort of)

All of Connie Walker's shepherding life, he has made it a point to go where his "sheep" were; in rural

Minnesota, this might mean an occasional livestock auction.

One bright morning, Connie made sure that he had a good seat and vantage point at his first full-fledged cattle auction. This bigger-than-life fella with his two college degrees who had "decked" the Minnesota heavyweight champ and attained near "All-American" status, found himself shoulder-to-shoulder with the steely-eyed, raw-boned professionals known as good-ole-boy Minnesota cattlemen and farmers. (Picture, if you will, a salmon in the middle of the Mojave Desert.)

During a period of time while things were a little less frantic, several of Connie's parishioners (out of the sight of the auctioneer) caught Connie's attention by shouting and waving at him. Connie, always ready to acknowledge his fellow man, waved back. The auctioneer dropped the gavel—and Connie had bought a heifer.

The ringleader of the crew that had set Connie up bought the bovine from Connie. That fellow, by the way, was Eddie Neumann, who had the distinction of once beating Walter Mondale in a school election—the only election Mondale ever lost—until Ronald Reagan.

The Lighter Side of Even the Most Negative Happenings of Parish Life

Since the earliest days of college (and continuing to this day), Connie has had a deep-rooted interest—and compassion for—the ministry of Alcoholics Anonymous. Even at Shiloh Lutheran there was a need for this ministry.

One evening the Walkers received a call from a dear lady of the congregation needing to talk to Connie about her husband. It seems that the dear soul had been doing very well with his battle against the liquid addiction; however, there appeared, sadly, to be a major slip.

Connie, of course (in spite of sloppy weather), immediately put on his five-buckle boots, a brand new (and stylish) topcoat, and headed in the direction of the distressed family's farm. Upon arriving, he was greeted by the wife and listened as she explained how well her husband had been doing. "However," she said, "with major financial reversals and mounting pressures, he has returned to his old ways—in a big way. In fact," she added, "he has bottles hidden everywhere. Even now he's down by the pig pens with a bottle."

Connie lost little time slogging through the mud to the pens. Sure enough, there was the dear, tormented soul with a quart of Four Roses whiskey—half gone. Connie was saddened at the thought of this wonderful little farm and the hard times that had so recently come about.

"Give me that bottle, dear friend," Connie gently demanded, but, "I will not," came the reply.

"You're doing harm to your family and yourself," Connie said, while all the while moving ever closer with no regard to the slush of mud and pigsty décor in which they were standing.

"Pastor, I've got a big mouth," said the parishioner, "I've poured 160 acres down this throat." While saying his piece, the wayward soul was making an ill-advised and threatening move toward Connie.

Rather than using his very advanced pugilistic abilities against the inebriated warrior, Connie decided to take the bottle from him. The sludge caused the two of them to lose their balance. The wrestling match that ensued lasted for several minutes before Connie was able to liberate the bottle of Four Roses. Connie then uncapped the bottle and poured the contents onto the soggy ground.

The miscreant rose to his knees yelling, "Stop that, Pastor, stop that! It's a sin, do you hear? That's made from fine pure grain and there are millions of people starving!"

Up to this point, Connie had won the day—at the expense of his brand new five-buckle boots and very stylish topcoat. After ministering to the family, however, it was time to go home.

As Connie approached the parsonage, lovely Ann was standing at the door. "Conrad Walker, don't you dare come into this house like that! Go hose yourself off." Her presence blocked the entrance—all five foot tall of her. Sure enough, the Shepherd of Shiloh, the indomitable heavyweight champion, hosed.

A Place to Call Home

Connie and Ann were blessed with the last two of their five children, Tim and Gracia, during the Elmore years, daughter Miriam and son Randy having joined the family ranks earlier in St. Paul. What a wonderful blessing from God are Beverly, Miriam, Randall, Timothy and Gracia (the caboose). They are ever so appreciated and loved.

So much was Elmore home to the Walkers, it was established that should some catastrophic event call Connie and Ann simultaneously home to God the Father, with the legal papers all in place, the children would always have a Christian home and loving care.

Blessed are Maynard and Madonna Gjerde, home for Beverly; Tom and Opal Wicks, opening their arms to Miriam; Anola Larson Hove and Ted and Judy Weise a beacon for Randy; Ralph and Esther Mastin, along with

Ted and Judy Weise for Tim; and finally, very special friends Myrl and Mavis Stenzel and Eldon and Pat Larson opening their home and hearts to Gracia.

Even though the Walkers traveled the world while in the U.S. Army, they made every attempt to have the children stay in their second home for a week each year. When each youngster reached his/her eighteenth birthday, a letter of profound "thank you" was sent to the dear friends who were willing to "stand-in-the-gap" should the need arise. Even though each of the children now have families of their own, this kind of love has been a memorable blessing for each of them.

One of the high watermarks of warmth and care during these cherished days in Elmore were the delightful neighboring pastors. The prince of pastors was my close neighbor, Pastor Kitzmann, of Trinity Lutheran Missouri Synod. He and his beloved wife had many sons, all servants of our Lord and one who is a pastor. They have one daughter, Lois, at that time a missionary nurse in India. She met, fell in love, and wed a fellow missionary, Paul Howe. They were blessed with a beautiful servanthood family. Paul become a prima parish pastor and then was later called to be a U.S. Army chaplain. He was the very best of the best of our shepherd/pastor chaplains.

Hebrews 2:12. "I will proclaim thy name to my brothers; In full assembly I will sing thy praise."-NEB

Finally, the Walker family will never forget one particular Easter Sunrise Service while at Shiloh Lutheran. The church was packed. Ann and the five very young (and exuberant) Walkers were ushered to the front pew. (*JWW note*: Young mothers with several close-aged toddlers will understand the tonnage that accompanies mom at all outings.)

Almost predictably, toward the middle of the service a small scuffle broke out between the boys (Randy and Tim). Gracia, being a babe in arms, of course required a healthy stack of diapers at all times (in the days before disposables).

All at once, a double handful of the cotton appliances were hurled skyward only to come floating back down (in Connie's view) as white doves, landing in an open field. One found a home, behind Ann, draped over the head of the congregation's most senior deacon, Matt Teigland.

Following the service, as Connie greeted each of the attendees at the door, he tried to tell Deacon Matt how sorry he was for the incident. The response was, "Pastor, don't worry about it. It could have been worse—the diaper could have been *loaded*!"

The five years at Elmore, Minnesota, were a blessing for the Walker family, and the Walker family was a blessing for Elmore.

As Connie prepared for a new and exciting chapter in his life, it was apparent that his time of shepherding at Shiloh Lutheran, unlike the diaper, *was* loaded!

IT DOESN'T GET ANY BETTER THAN THIS

CHAPTER 6

THIS IS THE ARMY. DIFFERENT? YOU BET!

Ezekiel 37:10. " . . . they came to life and rose to their feet, a mighty host."-NEB

Philippians 4:4, 6-7. "I wish you all joy in the Lord . . . The Lord is near; have no anxiety, but in everything make your requests known to God in prayer . . . Then the peace of God, which is beyond our utmost understanding, will keep guard over your hearts and your thoughts, in Christ Jesus."-NEB

(*JWW note:* The military years define Connie Walker as much or more than any other. Connie lived them so I'm going to sit back and let him relive them.)

The beloved families of Elmore's Shiloh Lutheran fed us very well all of the time we were there. With each home visit (after devotion, the reading of God's Word, prayer, and the singing of a hymn) they would serve coffee and a large piece of pie (whatever was in season), along with a piece of cheese and a scoop of tasty ice cream.

With this regimen (and there were a lot of visitations), extra poundage came on the frame. Vigorous exercise has always been a regular part of me, i.e., jogging, push-ups and sit-ups, but all of the goodies still packed on the extra weight. I generally made some headway, confronting any additional tonnage; however, the "call" to active duty was abrupt, swift, and sharp.

We drove through the welcoming gates of Fort Campbell, Kentucky, the first day of September 1962. My dear Lady Ann noticed several Airborne soldiers (who were in excellent physical condition) out on their daily run. Looking over at *big* me, she asked with obvious concern, "Are you going to make it?" She had clearly echoed the thoughts of countless souls upon entering the gates of the 101st (Screaming Eagles) Airborne Division.

After signing for and moving into quarters, I began the strong physical conditioning program. It was to be a regular part of life—particularly as I prepared for Airborne School at Fort Benning, Georgia.

While I was getting adjusted and giving chaplain coverage to Division Headquarters Company (a place of duty and preparedness for jump school), the division chaplain, Lieutenant Colonel Thomas Waldie, called me in for a quick briefing. Chaplain Waldie (one of the legends of Airborne chaplaincy) stated, "Connie, there are two ways to become jump qualified. One way is the regular jump school and the awarding of the silver wings. The other is one combat jump—and you are awarded the wings."

He went on to say, "Presently, it looks like it will be the latter, as we've been alerted to a potential jump into Cuba. I'll have a couple of soldiers take you to the back steps of this building, and they will prepare you to exit an aircraft—and on how to do a PLF (parachute landing fall)."

It was a breathtaking moment as I went to the back steps to learn how to do a PLF. The main position that my Lady Ann and I took was on our knees in prayer!

The next step was to check out all of the necessary combat jumping gear and equipment. We readied for the worst, but thankfully that urgent time passed without the combat jump into Cuba.

I was then assigned to the 502nd Battle Group with Chaplain William Froschner (a phenomenal chaplain/ pastor) and soon thereafter, with Chaplain (Monsignor) John McCullagh—a great man of God. He was a faithful priest from Brooklyn, New York. A lifelong and deep friendship and a trusting relationship sprang forth. We worked as a splendid team in the "Five-0-Duece" Battle Group. (*JWW note:* During the final days of this book's preparation, Father John McCullagh was called home to the Heavenly Father.)

It was a true blessing and special thrill to have dear friends from my Luther Seminary days awaiting us at Ft. Campbell: Chaplain LeRoy Ness and his beautiful and bright spouse, Evelyn.

LeRoy put me on the running and working out regimen immediately. He used wisdom and vigor as my key trainer. Each day, he slowly built up the run, the push-ups, sit-ups, chin-ups, and pull-ups until I was at that place in physical prowess that one could easily master the physical training test for Airborne School.

Soon after I finished jump school at Ft. Benning, Georgia, and I returned to Ft. Campbell, our new division chaplain arrived, Chaplain LTC Holland Hope, a most outstanding senior pastor/chaplain. He was a strong leader and an authentic, godly man. True, he was a hard-core disciplinarian, but one always knew where one stood and his standards were pristine. It was a special gift to be trained and mentored by this outstanding Methodist pastor/chaplain.

Physical readiness and training were maintained by regular visits to the Post gym—not to mention all of the 502nd unit runs and workouts.

First Sergeant Ted Arthur was a master soldier, trainer, and mentor. He was our First Shirt (1st Sergeant) and a very sure and steady influence. As our friendship and trust increased, First Sergeant Arthur used me as a teammate in assisting our soldiers in their lives of discipline.

Soldiers up for disciplinary action for misdeeds and lacking in motivation were offered an Article No. 15 (Uniform Code of Military Justice)—or to work out with 1st Sgt. Ted Arthur. The latter included a six-mile run. The First Sergeant led the way and I brought up the rear, assuring that the troops made the run—with an occasional stop to "push-up Kentucky." This increased motivation and special discipline gave errant troops a fresh beginning. This type of training we did for several years. A fast and lasting friendship was in place. (*JWW note*: At this point, I thought I would give Connie a bit of a break while we spend some time with the sergeant major.)

Ted Arthur has long since retired to Florida with his wonderful spouse Marlene. Ted (a published writer himself) is one of the literally dozens of respondents world over from Connie's past who have sent me encouragement, anecdotes, praise (for Connie), and warm thanks for becoming involved with putting forth this book.

Ted, having had a long relationship with Connie, sent me enough material for a small book in and of itself. There are stories of daring-do and moments of sentimental remembrance. There are some stories so personal that I shall leave them for other writings and perhaps for other writers. The feeling one gets through all of the histrionics, however, is an existence of mutual and deep respect.

Two tales from Ted give some insight into how the two of them in tandem might be:

Division got this big, ole long-legged one star assigned named Ryan. He was in charge of training, so all those colonels commanding outfits feared his wrath. We had heard stories about how tough he was, so naturally, when "Moose" (a private name for Connie, while Ted was known as "Wolf" or "Wuff") and I tangled with him, we expected dire results.

During the daily lunchtime six-miler, being an eccentric cuss, I wore only four items: dog tags, sox, jump boots, and a doggone red bathing suit. My reasoning was—it's snowing out. The troops are all in sweat-gear, bitchin' and cussin' that the ole bald-headed Wolf would run 'em in this weather. It would soon dawn on them, "How can we complain? Look at him! He'll freeze to death. And then—we'll be rid of him!" Nobody wanted to miss that!

On this particular day, I am at the head of the file of 18 "meatballs," the Moose, and Chaplain Charlie Watters. As we're running along through the falling snow, we see a big ole star on the license plate of a sedan bearin' down on us from the other direction. All that I could see were two huge eyeballs pasted against the sedan's window, taking in the scene as it sped by. I knew, without a doubt, that he was gonna turn around. I told Moose to keep on 'truckin'.

"No, Wolf," he says, "I'm the ranking man. I am not going to let you be my cannon fodder."

"Listen, sir—it's my run. He ain't gonna understand that the chaplain is punishin' a bunch o' duds. Believe me, I'm our only chance. Just keep on truckin'.'"

SCREEEEEEECH! The sedan stops beside us. I fall out, standin' tall as this big one star climbs out.

"Sir! First Sergeant Ted Arthur reports to the general, Sir! I am HQ, 2nd Brigade First Sergeant, Sir!"

"What in the hell is the meaning of this spectacle?"

"Sir! I am runnin' 18 duds in lieu of court martial or Article 15, makin' soldiers of them, Sir!"

He looked at me with interest, takin' in my red bathing suit. "So how far do you run them?"

I answered, "Six miles, Sir—every day. If they get back in time, they EAT. If they fall out, they STARVE, Sir!" I thought that I detected a slight smile.

"How often do you stop, Top?"

"Once, Sir."

"At the end?"

"At the end, Sir."

He lost control, threw back his head and laughed until tears melted the snow. "Well, hell! Don't let me hold up such a well-oiled machine. Hit it."

I saluted him, and hit it!

This is just one of dozens of anecdotes that solidified the early days of this strong friendship. Sure enough, as time went by, Wolf got promoted and went one way, and Connie got promoted and went another. But, of course, this was the Army, and other assignments would come along. In fact, years later, at West Point . . . Ted picks it back up.

Well, Sir! Moose gets assigned to Fort Hamilton, New York, the Chaplains School. Here I am an influential member of the Corps of Cadets, and the predictable question comes.

"Do you think you might be able to get tickets on the 50-yard line for the always highly touted Army/Navy football game?"

So here we all are—Moose, Ann, Marlene and I—sitting on the 50 enjoying the game. I had scrounged some extra tickers for Moose, and he had generously given them to some of the chaplain students from the school, and they were all sitting on the row in front of us.

We should have figured that wasn't coffee in the big thermos, which one of Moose's majors was periodically lifting to his lips to fend off the freezing weather. The contents of the thermos became obvious, however, when all of a sudden a Navy player intercepted a pass and ran it close to 100 yards for a TOUCHDOWN!

After the commotion subsided and everyone returned to their seats, the 50-yard line spectators were relatively quiet when one major leaped to his feet, brandishing the thermos, raising his hands beseechingly, to the heavens. "There is no GOD!" he screams! "There is no GOD!"

Now, there are a lot of big wheels that occupy the 50-yard line during the Army/Navy game from a place like West Point. A big buzz went up from the stands. "Who is this guy?"

When he turned around and faced the spectators, they could see his chaplain's insignia. Someone behind us says to a companion, "Oh. We must have misunderstood him. I thought he said there is no God. I probably need a hearing aid!"

Connie, holding his head in his hands said, "We all do sometimes."

(*CNW note:* "We are not the good, but thanks be to God we are the forgiven!")

Humor is Captivating

We had a big, strong soldier who had a dynamic and dynamite conversion to our Lord. We deeply rejoice in the newness of life experiences for our beloved soldiers; however, this newly-inspired soldier lacked in the realm of wisdom. He would start preaching at the most inopportune times: in the mess hall line, in the laundry, on the bus, in the library, and in the aircraft while in flight. He, in fact, became a danger for the troops because he spoke while the jump master was giving voice commands and hand signals, all the while at 1000 feet and 150 knots per hour.

He yelled, "If you don't know the Lord, the parachute will burn all up and you will fall to the ground and be killed!" This caused several new jumpers fresh from jump school to refuse to jump—a serious offense, for a jumper.

The jump master wisely reached me at the Airborne Chapel by field phone. He told me the story and said that the three refusal troops were on their way in from the aircraft to the commander for serious disciplinary action.

I hurried to the commander's office, told the story (as I knew it), and volunteered to jump with the three in the early morning. So, after their commander's firm talk, the three came to the Airborne Chapel. They shared their scary story, and we talked. As we became trusting friends, I suggested that we consider the misguided, converted soldier's words about life and death and the fear of dying.

I told these tremendous soldiers that we fear death no more than we do our beds at night, because our Lord Jesus has overcome the enemies and tyrants of sin, death, and the power of the evil one.

They rejoiced in the message, believed it, and agreed to jump together the next morning. They had a great Airborne operation—a great jump. When these soldiers hit the ground for their sixth time, they leaped like gazelles. (Five jumps were required to qualify as a paratrooper at the Airborne School at Fort Benning.)

They were real happy soldiers: happy in their uniforms, in the U.S. Army Paratroopers, and happy to be assured as believers in our Lord. They had the victory and became true and balanced leaders in the faith community at the Airborne Chapel.

It was during this tour that I met a great Airborne trooper, Nicholas Worth. He was a sharp and strong soldier who became a devout Christian soldier. We became, and are, fast friends in our Lord. Nick went on to Hollywood, California, and became one of the very best and gifted character actors to this very day.

(*JWW note:* A few words from Nick Worth. Thanks, Nick.)

I first met Connie while serving as an army paratrooper with the 101st Airborne Division. He was Captain Walker then; the date that I met

Connie face to face was 15 February 1963, the day that I accepted Jesus Christ as my personal Lord and Savior. He came to visit me in the Fort Campbell hospital where I was recovering from a second-degree burn on my right leg. Connie was the first person I told of my conversion.

No one had such an impact on my Christian walk in the military as did Chaplain Connie Walker. His power to communicate the Living Christ from the pulpit, his physical prowess and strength, made me see the *man,* Jesus Christ, in a different light than I had ever seen....Chaplain Walker, to me, was the epitome of "all-man." He represented what I wanted to be. He was a perfect example of how and what my relationship with Christ should be.

Connie Walker has been a true and faithful brother in Christ, a real intercessor, and a prayer warrior like no other. How I thank God in Christ Jesus for my conversations with Connie and the notes of encouragement that I receive from him.

Humor Follows the Adventurous
(and those who can recognize it—no matter what)

Connie related this story with both compassion and a twinkle in his eye.

First Sergeant John T. Hutson sent a large and strong two-hundred-plus pounder to be counseled by the chaplain—yes, to Connie's office.

The soldier had gone "wild" the night before in a local eatery. He thought his sandwich was not nearly large or thick enough, so he proceeded to enter the kitchen to fulfill his hunger desire and punch out the chef.

The military police returned him to his company. The errant soldier then punched out a fellow soldier in the mid-morning, and that's when the first sergeant sent him to Connie's office. Two fellow chaplains were in the next office talking and coordinating, both very effective and godly men: Chaplain Ralph Goff and Chaplain Frank (Francis) Ligget. Also present was my talented chaplain's assistant, Lloyd E. Leyh, assistant and friend. He was always nearby and even recognized as a potential leader by First Sgt. Ted Arthur.

The disturbed soldier charged across the office to punch out and clobber the chaplain. (As previously stated, Chaplain Connie Walker spent many years in the ring as a heavyweight boxer and a boxing coach.)

Connie yelled at the troop, "Hold your place!" but he continued his charge and tried to nail Connie. The otherwise friendly "mastodon" with a cross on his collar threw the wild bull of the misguided back against the wall. It rattled loudly. The young soldier charged again. This time, Connie hooked him solidly in the nose and the diaphragm. He again smashed into the wall—this time, on his way down. The two neighboring chaplains came over and saw the soldier wiggling in his slumber, with his bloody, crooked nose.

Chaplain Liggett called the first sergeant and said "Big fight! Big fight!" That's all he could seem to say. The first sergeant arrived quickly with four strong Airborne soldiers and loudly declared, "How bad is Chaplain Walker hurt?" After observing his fallen warrior, he looked at Connie with scorn and asked, "What the hell did you do to my soldier?"

The young, slumbering warrior was hospitalized but did well and was released in several days. (Oh, yes, before his release, he punched out the psychiatrist.) He did, however, settle down and came to say farewell to

Connie at the chapel. He departed the Army with a less-than-desirable discharge. In his farewell to Connie, he said, "Chaplain, I'm a new man. You truly 'kicked the hell' out of me!"

Cherished Memories (In Connie's Words)

My family and I remember the most extraordinary and lavish Thanksgiving dinners in our 502nd mess halls during our assignment at Ft. Campbell. Our mess sergeants, from our point of view, were the world's best. They made presentations that are not duplicated by the four-star chefs in great hotels.

Literally dozens of turkeys and hams were on display along with massive fruit arrangements. There were mountains of vegetables and all kinds of nuts, candies, onions, olives, carrots, tomatoes, avocados, figs, cranberry preparations, and bread dressings with and without sage. There were sweet potatoes and several kinds of potatoes (baked, mashed, and some cooked with parsley and butter). The pies, oh, the pies: pumpkin, apple, mincemeat, pecan, and apple crisp, and all manner of toppings. (*JWW note:* Connie and I have worked for several years on this writing and this is the most excited I've seen him!)

My family would dine in one huge Thanksgiving mess hall. I would stay as long as possible but had seven mess halls to visit over the course of a couple of hours to have a Thanksgiving prayer. I ate well but was highly mobile.

The mess sergeant always wanted us to take food home for our large and growing family, a tremendous and blessed memory. I frequently sang a portion of the Thanksgiving prayer: "Be present at our table Lord, Be here and everywhere adored. These mercies bless and grant that we, may strengthen for Thy service be!"

(*JWW note:* The Thanksgiving reminiscing caused Connie to reflect further on the family aspect of this period.)

When we came on active duty as a chaplain (captain) from the Minnesota National Guard, the salary was half of what we were receiving from the kind people at Shiloh Lutheran Church. We had to make all of our funds stretch, and Ann was a master at so doing.

The social events were not "come if you would like" but were full of expectation that you would be present. With our precious five children, we frequently used the post nursery for social events, chapel events, and our continual courting. This, for us, was a heavy expense. Frugality was part of our lives.

With that as such, we always found a tremendous family outing that would cost very little or nothing. Pennyrile Park, near Fort Campbell, was such a place. It made available to us picnic areas, water sports, hiking, biking, flowers, plants, and trees, etc. We thrilled with each family visit.

On post we always found, after a search and family meeting, a tree that would be our family tree. There we would play and pray, gather leaves for home coloration and centerpieces, and make it a game area. It was a time for great fun, imagination, and memory development for both parents and children.

I would even bring home extra "C" rations from the field that I did not consume. What a treat! Ann continued to sew much of the children's clothing. They looked super and superb—even though we were so poor. If trips around the world were fifty cents, we couldn't get out of sight.

Back to Work

Our units and troops took all of our priority time, but we did allow ourselves time to periodically preach in area churches, with the permission of our division chaplain and unit commander.

The area churches seemed delighted to have a "Leapin' Deacon" paratrooper-type chaplain/pastor in their pulpits. It was a Gospel enterprise, but also a grand relational encounter with the civilian community. Our Lord Christ was proclaimed wherever we served.

We had a radical trust that the Holy Spirit was powerfully active and winning people for the Kingdom of God. It's true that we bring a sense of urgency, sacrifice, meaning and purpose wherever we go. The chaplain is ideally suited to visit most area churches because he/she serves people of all denominations and backgrounds.

During the entire tour and mission at Fort Campbell, a major issue was time-time-time. Personal pastoral contact was forever and ongoing. The contact was with the soldier and family members as pastor, counselor, mentor, friend, and shepherd. Shepherding the flock is always primary!

The chaplain must always maintain a sure sense of mission, "To bring soldiers to the Lord, and the Lord to soldiers." This pastoral/shepherding mission is a non-negotiable. This is our calling and shepherding attitude. This is a trait that God gives us, no matter if we are in the early part of our ministry or as a senior chaplain. (*JWW note:* Connie tells a charming story below about one of the pitfalls of serious family shepherding during those years.)

A young sergeant came in and said, "Chaplain, I need help. All of this field duty and one mission after another—well, my family is nearly falling apart. My wife and I aren't making it."

I invited the couple in for pastoral counseling and active caring. After a couple of meetings (their home was formerly in the Caribbean and had some serious involvement with voodoo), the wife perceived that I was tilting toward the soldier. She became angry, and along with a couple of voodoo-practicing neighbors, made a G.I. Joe-style doll of the offending chaplain (me, cross and all) and proceeded to drive a huge pin through the doll. Ho-boy!

The young sergeant and I had an early morning ATT parachute jump—a hard-core Army Training Test involvement. We were on the same aircraft—the same manifest. Well, he got a case of the "big eyes" and said, "Chaplain, I don't believe in that stuff—voodoo and all, but I'm not going to remain on the same aircraft with you." Prior to the jump, the sergeant was able to pull off an eleventh-hour change of aircraft jump manifest. We both jumped (from separate aircraft) and had a fine jump. In fact, I was rejoicing over a rather easy (soft) landing.

I met the sergeant in the drop zone and told him it was time we went to prayer in Jesus' name to wash out, yes, *flush* out, any further influences of voodoo curses and such. We prayed and he rejoiced with me. As we came to the assembly point, I secured a field phone and spoke to his spouse (who was in post housing) saying, "Dear sister, if you continue with cursing and false god practices, you are going straight to hell."

She and her husband came in after our field exercise. We visited deeply and prayed, and she was elated to return to her Lord and her husband's Christian faith life.

I was given the chaplain doll, needle pierced and all. I kept that thing for a while as a reminder that we follow

the loving and kind Heavenly Father—the One True
God—the Covenant God who blesses so that we can be
blessings, and his fresh new call, "Follow Me!"

The Preacher Surfaces—
But, Then Again, That's Who He Is.

(*JWW note:* Connie often lapses into a teaching/
preaching mode in the middle of reminiscing!)

The pastoral duty and mission during those years
with the 101st Airborne was absolutely demanding,
blessedly phenomenal, and awe inspiring. There was
newness, and new names were forever being written in
the Book of Life by God's great grace, mercy, and
shepherding.

Excitement and adventure was par excellence, but
the undergirding and foundation was our wondrous
Covenant God, Savior, Lord Jesus, and mighty Holy
Spirit calling us and sending us on mission. This is done
to win, hold, develop, and disciple soldiers and families
in the faith life. Yes, we are a called and sent people,
rooted and winged.

It's a poignant thought—a captivating thought. It is,
further, dreadful to think of going through life never
sent, called, or summoned to a great task/tasks/or
mission. Our Lord's call is a holy maneuver where the
Lord's will is lived out in a person's life, in our environment, and culture.

The Lord calls us to a sense of purpose, a wondrous
mission, a rendezvous, if you will, with meaning and
"reason for." Christ Jesus calls us to "Follow Me!" This
is an exalted commission. This amplifies each soldier,
yes, each person's importance and unlimited value.
Each soldier is called—sent—as a leader in the Kingdom of God enterprises.

We are called to follow him. We are sent to declare in word and deed, his love in all of its forms and cares, and we praise him for such trust in us. Certainly we ought to thank, praise, serve, obey, and honor him! It's a life packed with purpose and meaning, love, and authentic care. It is truly the living out of Genesis 12:1-3, "I will bless you to be blessings."

It is covenant love. The Hebrew word is "Hesed": his steadfast love, his loving kindness surrounds and sustains us in all our missions. It again holds forth in St. Mark 12 and St. Matthew 22: "Love the Lord your God with all your heart, with all your soul, and with all your mind, and with all your strength," and "Love your neighbor as you love yourself." "No other commandment is greater than these," declares our Lord Jesus!

Connie Never Loses Sight of Family

The steady and hard work, firm physical conditioning, bold training life, and the vast sparks of jubilance seasoned the mix to be just right. Our deep, trusting, and exciting family life, however, continued to flourish, to grow, and to deepen. We always carved out primary family time and meaningful adventures in love and living in growth together.

Ever since the first days of our marriage, Ann and I celebrated a family night evening together and with the addition of each child, it became more alive, meaningful, and robust. Family life together was just that—a deepening life of joy and love together.

As the children grew and school events came about, we vigorously kept our family night and fun time in place, and we made it actual and real. A celebration atmosphere was present and a love attitude prevailed with and for the children.

Every second or third week (depending on the need), we would have a family council meeting to talk over: How are we making it together? Where are we mostly getting along? Where are we missing the mark? Where are we hurting? What can we do about it?

We would first underline our family strengths, then we would move to any weaknesses that needed special attention and care. What can we do to make life more blessed and more meaningful for one another?

Over the years, the young people developed great skills at assisting one another in weak areas and refined their own personal insights and spiritual maturity. They became champions on what needed to be done to make life more enjoyable and less hurtful.

The entire family was growing in Godly wisdom and caring. As time went on, they all became surgeons, so-to-speak, in their own right, knowing that they had the scalpel in their own hands to do healing surgery on "Ish" (themselves) first—then the other family members, within the realm of healthy relationship.

The theme was set in that we had a strong and daily devotional life together. Each would take their turn to lead the family. They would select the scripture and the hymns. They would lead in prayer and the closing with the Apostle's Creed and/or the Lord's Prayer.

If their friends happened to be in our home, they were invited to join us if they so desired. The strengthening of the family in the Lord and in daily pragmatic things and happenings steadily progressed. Their growth in all areas of life was like a vast and beautiful symphony! Praise God!

Connie Also Never Loses Sight of the Army

The U.S. Army moved away from the battle group design (during the latter days of my Ft. Campbell assignment) back to the brigade and with new alignments, assignments were changed. I moved from North Chapel to Central Chapel and from battle group to the 502nd, 2nd Battalion.

Chaplain (Fr.) John McCullagh remained my senior chaplain/pastor and our trust and friendship flourished in a grand and prayerful way. He was a pastoral leader par excellence. He went on to become Senior Chaplain to the New York Police Department of about 40,000 police officers. Wow! We are thankful that he is at home with the Heavenly Father, but he is sorely missed!

Early on while at Central Chapel, Chaplain Robert Crick joined our team upon his return from Germany. A deep and abiding friendship and fellowship developed in trust. We studied God's Word and had long seasons of prayer together, and we shared in worship. Soldiers of all ages and ranks and their family members responded in a heartening and glorious way.

In fact, our joint ministry so moved the people that congregates had to arrive early in order to be seated. We rejoiced in such a blessed response to the Gospel. Our counseling load was heavy. We had to be helped (periodically) by our Division Chaplain Hope, his distinguished NCO "Tip" Tippins, and the rest of his staff because the soldiers' response was so pronounced.

Chaplain Crick and I served together in the 101st, then the 173rd Airborne, and then at Fort Benning, Georgia. We conducted preaching and baptismal services in all of these places—what a blessed and trusted friend. Chaplain Crick is an outstanding Christian leader. He has gone on to become the endorsing agent with the Church of God at Cleveland, Tennessee. Under his leadership, they went from several dozen chaplains to several thousand strong.

LIFE'S CARDINAL RULE:
"RELAX TO THE POINT OF CONTROL."

The pastoral chaplain team at Central Chapel was top drawer: Chaplain (Fr.) John McCullagh, our chief, Chaplain (Major) Ralph Goff, a great Southern Baptist pastor; and Chaplain (Fr.) Charlie Watters (much more about him elsewhere in this book) who also joined our team.

Chaplain Phil Johnston, an outstanding Episcopalian priest, was aboard as was the most vibrant and caring Chaplain Robert Harley, a Southern Baptist and the stalwart engineer battalion chaplain, and Richard Heim, a Covenant/Lutheran. They always did a sure and steady job as chaplain/pastor and friend of the soldier. All were sharp, creative leaders in the kingdom of God—along with our faithful, multi-skilled chaplains' assistants.

One of the many fine chaplain assistants that I have been blessed with over the years was Specialist Lloyd Leyh. Lloyd was a strong young leader then and has become a lifelong close friend. One story from those early days always comes to mind during times of reflection.

We had a large Airborne wedding at the chapel. The groom, a spirited paratrooper, was so excited that he failed to take the keys out of his car before securing it.

After the meaningful and life-sharing vows of marriage, there was a fine reception on the lawn hosted by the chapel. All was joyous and gleeful until the newlyweds attempted to be off on their honeymoon.

The keys were locked securely in the car. Frustration was paramount. In a rather conspiratorial way, Specialist Leyh said to me, "Chaplain, if you won't think any less of me, I can get into that car—quickly!" He did. All were happy. No questions were ever asked.

Another drama starring Lloyd and me (these are two stories taken from a dozen or so) was when we went quail and squirrel hunting in the woods, not too far from Clarksville, Tennessee. It was a beautiful day. The woods were exceptionally clear and clean. We chased a couple of squirrels into a large hardwood tree with a hole near the bottom.

Lloyd said, "Let's smoke them out!" Unwise, but we made a small and smoky fire as our purpose, of course, was to harvest them for dinner. A breeze arose, and the fire spread. I ran quickly to a nearby farmhouse and borrowed two five-gallon buckets. A small creek was close at hand and, thankfully, we extinguished the fire. It scared us!

We left the squirrels to their own chuckling life and went further into the deep forest looking for quail. To our surprise, we stumbled upon an unauthorized liquor still. We heard rifles being cocked. Two of the entrepreneurial merchants came forward and checked us out. We were in Army fatigues. "Are you soldiers?" one man asked. "Yes," I responded. His companion looked at my collar and asked, "Are you a chaplain?" Again I responded in the affirmative. "Do we have your word that you will not give away our location or business?" We both answered that they had our word, and we eagerly departed. Lloyd and I agreed we'd had enough hunting for one day!

(*JWW note:* My turn for an observation.) It was during this time that Connie first started singing the praises of the marvelous noncommissioned officers and potential NCOs that served as chaplains' assistants. The dedication, commitment, and high standards required of / and maintained by these outstanding soldiers earned Connie's unyielding respect during the entire span of his long and glorious military career.

Connie maintains that these fine soldiers always furthered the lay ministry in the military to the highest degree of excellence. Several of these outstanding men and women soldiers (at Connie's urging and mentoring) went on to become outstanding chaplains, all serving with honor and pride, while others returned to the civilian world to become strong lay leaders in their home church communities. (*JWW note:* Back to Connie.)

Important Sermon Series—Jump Commands

Early on, while in the 101st Airborne Division, I put together a series of messages that have served me (and Airborne soldiers) well over the years. Using the eight Jump Commands and the appropriate Biblical parallels, I wrote the following titled sermons:

1. "Get Ready"—Luke 12:35-37; Psalm 46; Hebrews 10:19; Matthew 24:36-44. "Get ready for a deeper walk with the Lord; all that we have prepared and trained for is at hand. The ultimate and urgent time is here!"

2. "Stand Up"—Romans 5:1-2; John 19:25-30; Hebrews 4 and 12; Psalms 1 and 27. "Let's do it! Stand up for him who is the Way, Truth, Life."

3. "Hook Up"—I Thessalonians 5:17; Ephesians 6:18; Psalm 23; Luke 9:28. "Vital life line. Prayer is Holy ground; Holy Conversation."

4. "Check Static Line"—Philippians 4:6; I John 5; Psalm 27. "Vigorous check. Extreme care of those around you. The body of the concerned. The church."

5. "Check Equipment"—Ephesians 6:10-20. "Check from top to bottom. Put on the whole armor of God."

6. "Sound off Equipment Check"—Psalm 107:2; I Peter 1:3-5; Psalm 103:1-5. "Let the redeemed of the Lord say so."

7. "Stand in the Door"—John 10:7-13. "I am the door."

8. "Go!"—Matthew 28:16-20. "Great Commission. Go into all nations . . . I am with you always, even to the end of the world."

The Airborne soldiers resoundingly responded to these "Jump Command" messages, and it was fun and meaningful.

Training, Training, Training

During the years 1962-1966, we participated in some vital training operations:
* Swift Strike
* Desert Strike
* Operation One Shot
* Immediate Ready Force--Operations and training.

Each field training mission was filled with zest and high adventure living for our proud Airborne soldiers. "Swift Strike" was the name for the training mission in and around Newberry, South Carolina, and was such a memorable time.

As we jumped in, many of us landed in large watermelon fields. Soldiers are quick to realize when they have been given an unplanned gift—and a number of nice, ripe watermelons burst open when the paratroopers landed on them. They gleefully partook in some very sweet, tasty watermelon pieces as they hurried to the meeting and round-up area (unit assembly point). Please keep in mind that the South Carolina farmers were reimbursed for any damage or losses, to include watermelons.

It so happened that that particular area where we jumped was made up (largely) of Lutheran Christian farmers. These patriotic folks heard that a Lutheran pastor/chaplain was with the Airborne soldiers, and they were extra gracious to us. They rigged up their barns and made a "shower point" available to the troops during the training exercise. They further announced,

"Please have your Lutheran chaplain and about ten soldiers come up to the house for a Southern home-cooked meal." They always asked the chaplain to bless the meal in our Lord's saving name.

This welcome event was graciously repeated several times during the operation. The farmers' kindness prompted many of the Airborne officers and men to exclaim, "Man, that is a special kind of witness for those folks and their caring church." They really took seriously the Lord's command about loving your neighbor!

Each operation had many such poignant and memorable anecdotes, and we shall cherish them until the last days. Another humorous memory has its roots in operation "Desert Strike."

Our 101st Airborne Unit—the 502nd—was dropped into the rustic, rugged, and beautiful Mojave Desert. The only important item the desert did not have was water. When a water source was found, the desert flowers blossomed everywhere (simply beautiful).

In this very dry and hot place, soldiers each had two water canteens to carry them through to the next vital water point. On this training operation, once the paratrooper dropped in, he was a foot soldier. (I marched across the Mojave Desert with troops commanded by Captain Jonnie Britton, later to rise to a distinguished level of rank and leadership.)

We had all been cautioned about the large population of diamondback rattlesnakes and the smaller and swifter sidewinder snakes. We had to dispatch (kill) half a dozen large, poisonous snakes before getting off the drop zone.

One other concern that the paratroopers had was the large crop of big cacti that had sharp and piercing needles, as well as the more dangerous spanish sword cactus that could run you through—or give serious injury.

One of our tremendous and gifted young leaders, 1st Lt. Dean Learish, came in backwards on his parachute-landing fall and was unfortunate enough to receive several sharp stickers in his hindquarters (buttocks). A most able medic extracted the needles with a pair of pliers. While his hindquarters were exposed, one of our humorous soldiers yelled out, "Sir, we just killed half a dozen rattlesnakes coming off the DZ, so make sure you don't get bit in the rump! If that happens, you'll really find out who your friends are!" (At that time, immediate treatment for snakebite was to insert a small cut and suck the poison out.)

The soldier always finds ways to express humor.

The U.S. Army, like the Heavenly Father, prepared us well (Ephesians 6:10-20). Vietnam was looming bigger and bigger. We saw great NCOs and officers moving into Vietnam as advisors to South Vietnamese units. This was indeed serious and hazardous duty.

A Short Respite During Trying Times

The chaplain team encouraged Ann and me to take the whole family on a camping trip to the Smoky Mountains. It seemed like a good idea as school was out, and we had considerable leave time coming. The drive to the picturesque and inspirational Smoky Mountains was a family delight.

We arrived at the camping area in the Smoky Mountain National Park. We were given a nice grassy and, we thought, a splendid place to pitch our tent. It was a lower piece of terrain; just fine, if it didn't rain. We proceeded to set up our camp, air mattresses and all. We enjoyed a fine first evening cookout, and then, well, it began to rain, rain. Ann, with Beverly and Gracia, retreated to sleep in the back of the station wagon, while the rest of the kids and I settled down in the tent on our comfortable air mattresses on the ground.

At 1 A.M., several things awakened us: floating air mattresses and a deep, disquieting growling sound. A big brown bear was sitting on the edge of our tent eating goodies just stolen from folks parked behind us in a beautiful Air Stream travel home. As the bear made all manner of noises while eating and drinking (a gallon of milk, we later discovered), it began to occupy more and more of our tent area.

I tried to quietly comfort the children as they floated on their air mattresses. I zipped them up in their sleeping bags and tried to encourage them to be quiet and trust in the Lord. A couple of them responded, "We trust, Dad, but we're scared!"

At about that time, the person who had lost the food items came charging over beating two cooking pots together, trying to scare the bear off. I suppose that he had read a book saying that is one way to drive a bear out of your area. Unfortunately, the bear hadn't read the same book. The bear chased him back to his own quarters.

I remained inside the tent with a small axe, ready to do battle to protect the family if necessary, but the need thankfully never arose. The next day, the bear was found by the park rangers, tranquilized, and taken to a higher part of the park.

We endured a couple more days of rain, then headed back to Fort Campbell, if not rested, at least entertained with another adventure.

Shortly thereafter, the lid blew—the "Tonkin Bay" incident! Entire large American units were sent to Vietnam and the 173rd Airborne was the first U.S. Army Unit deployed to Bien Hoa.

Our great pastoral team was being sent to Vietnam—as individual replacements—then a bit later (after the build up) as battalion and brigade chaplains. Welcome to senior pastoral leadership.

When a Door Closes—Another Door Opens

The grand and fruitful tour with the 101st Airborne "Screaming Eagles" was coming to an end. We were alerted for orders to Vietnam and to the 173rd Airborne Brigade.

We are a praying family and, with many of our friends and neighbors at Fort Campbell, we devoutly and diligently brought them before the Lord in prayer. We knew that our time for a tour in hostile territory was quickly coming. Our preparation was within the regular and ordinary lifestyle of our family, seasoning all things in prayer in our Savior's name with a radical trust in his love and grace!

Orders came! Ann and I selected a great community as our home base while I was serving as chaplain/pastor in a most hostile environment. Our selection was Blue Earth, Minnesota, a tremendous community and the countyseat just north of where we served our first pastorate in Elmore, Minnesota.

Thus, Ann had some dear and blessed friends close by, and the children were in a happy and supportive place near their second homes and their second parents. This arrangement was of great comfort to Ann and me.

As another important element affecting our choice of home, Blue Earth had a rich and steadfast Christian support community of faith. During this time, our family belonged to Trinity Lutheran Church, a vibrant and boldly faithful body of Christ. Further, the dedicated teachers, educational facilities, and medical resources were outstanding, along with faithful officers of the law and well-trained, ready firemen. (Oh, yes, and great neighbors.)

Mark and Maria Lindberg and their five children were exceedingly helpful and shall long shine in our memories. Mark was the German teacher as well as the drivers' education instructor. He coached and taught Ann how to drive an auto. Maria was a caring and loving listener and friend to Ann all the time I served in dangerous and hostile territory.

Inevitably, it was time to catch my flight for the first leg of my journey to Vietnam. "Up and at 'em," 18 April 1966 at 0400 hours from Minneapolis—a season of prayer!—and arriving in Chicago at 0600. My dear mom and dad met me, and we had a fine breakfast together, a warm visit, and prayer. I then departed for Oakland, California.

I was able to visit the Berkley Campus in jump boots and uniform (unusual attire) and the Pacific Lutheran Seminary campus. At 1500 hours, we took off for Vietnam with stops in Hawaii, Guam, the Philippines, and finally Saigon. (*JWW note:* As the great W. C. Fields once said, "All things considered, I'd rather be in Philadelphia!")

CHAPTER 7

MY PIECE OF THE WAR

Ecclesiastes 3:8. ". . . a time for war and a time for peace."-NEB

Colossians 3:1-3. "Were you not raised to life with Christ? Then aspire to the realm above, where Christ is, seated at the right hand of God, and let your thoughts dwell on that higher realm, not on this earthly life. I repeat, you died; and now your life lies hidden with Christ in God."-NEB

(*CNW note:* Much of the following chapter is taken from my pastoral calendar and journal while on the move with the Sky Soldiers in Vietnam, hence its succinct outline style and character. It is a product produced on the battlefield.)

I arrived in Saigon on 21 April 1966. There was no grass growing under the feet of the people movers in the personnel section at that time so I was whisked immediately to Camp Alpha, where I signed in. Camp Alpha was a holding area, and from there you went to your assigned unit.

Chaplain (Fr.) John McCullagh, my dear and trusted friend, came and picked me up on 22 April and hand delivered me to our hooch (quarters) in Bien Hoa. I received a sure and quick briefing by Chaplain John McCullagh and outgoing Chaplain John Porter (a master proclaimer and pastor).

The next day, Sunday, 24 April, was my first worship service for the 17th Cavalry and the Second of the 503rd Airborne Battalion (BN). The Scripture lesson was the Gospel of St. John 10:11-16. The sermon theme was "The Good Shepherd." The hymns were "Come Thou Almighty King," "Holy, Holy, Holy," and "My Faith Looks up to Thee." (*JWW note:* Connie's personal library contains copies of virtually every service he conducted during his entire ministry.)

Then it was off in a chopper with Chaplain (Fr.) John McCullagh on an hour-long flight to Song Be sector in the northern-half of Phouc Long Province on an operation called "Denver."

The 173rd's task was to check the steady infiltration of Viet Cong into war zone "D." My task was to pastor our soldiers (of all ages and ranks) and make sure they had solid, steady, and sure shepherding pastoral support as they moved on with Operation Denver.

I was immediately thrust into a hostile combat environment. All past years of training would come front and center to a great degree in caring for the soldiers as chaplain, as pastor, and as spiritual leader. This was real; yes this was war—the several years of training under (and with) phenomenal NCOs, officers, and soldiers paid wondrous dividends by way of assisting in mighty ministry and survivability.

There was an awesome dimension while moving about as one of the chaplains in the 173rd Airborne Brigade (separate). I had the assurance that I was surrounded by "a great cloud of witnesses"—Hebrews 12:1—both the chaplains that had come and gone before me, and those champions of faith with whom I was privileged to be working and walking alongside ...never losing sight of the importance of the soldier, the soldier . . . the honored soldier!

Truly, one had a sense of walking on holy ground while on a vital and holy mission: To win, to hold, develop, and to disciple soldiers for the Lord and His family of believers, the people of God—the Church. The mission is compelling, demanding, and challenging beyond description. Daily, I thank and praise God for his call to be a pastor/chaplain. Following this, I am most thankful for the superb support and training by my seminary and church for their clear and bold Christian leadership.

A non-combat incident comes to mind: on 3 May a severe thunderstorm occurred and one of our young soldiers was hit by lightning while on a field phone. I was called in for prayer and comfort. Praise God, the young Airborne trooper turned out fine.

A steady stream of young soldiers and NCOs and young (as well as senior) officers asked for instruction in the Word and preparation for holy baptism. If a soldier so requested, I would have private holy communion and a deepening devotion and spirituality gift for the trooper. We found many desiring to grow in grace, holiness, and wisdom. Newness in the Lord is a most wonderful happening and experience. Yes, the Holy Spirit was mightily at work.

I always had an early morning devotion and holy communion before each operation. An example of this would be, on 4 May 1966, prior to Operation Dexter, our devotion centered on Titus 2:11-15, a most powerful and assuring portion of God's Word.

Operation Dexter was made up of several elements—all in torrential rains. Soldiers moved through heavy rains, rice paddies, and jungles for many hours, and still they were alert, ready, and oh, yes, very wet. It was a beautiful and striking area that one wanted to enjoy. The critical and hostile circumstances, however, kept one tensely alert and ready for any eventuality. We became aware and sensitive to flowers of all kinds and colors; the scene nearly captivated one—however, we had to press on. Even thirty-plus years later, the thought surfaces of such radical beauty and such terrible danger.

We came under sniper fire several times, and although our troops quickly solved the problem with return—and accurate—fire, the snipers continued their long-distance harassment. Praise God, we had a resupply by choppers, along with some most welcome warm chow for our soldiers.

Another note of importance: it was a distinct honor to serve side by side with the tough and highly trained, motivated, and trustworthy Australian and New Zealander soldiers during part of my tour in the 173rd Airborne. They increased in numbers and missions and formed their own prestigious command.

The next day (5 May '66) we moved all day through very heavy jungle; all of a sudden came an opening and a very well-groomed rubber plantation. A chopper was brought down by sniper fire, and although all escaped, the chopper was destroyed.

I helped carry a trooper with heat exhaustion out of the jungle. We prayed with and for him, using the Lord's Prayer and the 23rd Psalm, all the while cutting vines with machetes. It was exceedingly tough going. Again, beauty and danger co-mingled!

We ran into an area infested with large red biting ants—terrible! They bit as soon as they crawled on you (similar to the scourge of fire ants in the southwest USA).

On 6 May—a jubilant day—I received a most welcome letter from Ann and the children. It put a real bounce in my walk and my heart was aglow with thanksgiving. My brothers Don and Bill were also most faithful in sending warm and informative letters, real epistles of encouragement and faith!

On 8 May, morning devotion was a powerful promise of the Lord, John 16:5-15. Sky Soldiers are soldiers par excellence—tough and ready for the most difficult missions. They were full of deep appreciation to have their chaplain/pastor with them on company-sized moves.

The chaplain would generally move out with the company commander's folks. Out in front would be the point and weapons people, rotating the point; then would be the C.O. (Commanding Officer), his RTO, (communications person[s]), the senior medic, the chaplain and his assistant, the artillery forward observer and all our soldiers in front and behind us, the nerve center.

11-17 May

The mid-May operation was most difficult. The terrain was acutely tough, rugged beyond rugged, and many of the troops were ill affected. Some of the cliffs were sixty feet high, but we had to handle and negotiate them—and that we did! Boulders ripped loose every now and then and injured a dear Sky Soldier. We had to carry injured troops until we found openings, where we could call in Medivac or the Green Giant (an even larger helicopter with a powerful hoist system aboard).

At one point, I fell eighteen feet onto rocks but was most fortunate to come out with only a terribly sore lower back. (I still have some serious aftermath pain from that incident, but the need to remain with the dear troops was great and we pressed on.)

All during our jungle journey on these vital days, we were able to comfort our Sky Soldiers and discuss the most important things in their lives. This was a time of real value testing of what is important in life. We were dealing with a considerable number of life decisions. We were pastoral in our friendship, visits, and discussions—right in the middle of the rugged terrain and the hostile jungles of Vietnam. Our 173rd Airborne troops were full of humor, vigor, and hope for the future.

We were mightily relieved when an airlift (dustoff) picked up an injured soldier, but the very next day, again the sheer cliffs and super-rugged terrain caused a Sky Soldier to slip on vines and fall. We had to carry him for the rest of the day until we found an evacuation place. We were ever so thankful for the dustoff pilots and their medical teams.

The many thick vines were a real help as we descended some of the cliffs. The tired soldier was ever so open to share his life's dreams and hopes and the meaning of life in our Lord. "Truly, if we have a reason why, we can tolerate any how."—Viktor Frankel

Along with difficult terrain, heavy monsoon rains came several times a day, and we often were beyond being soaked. At night, we would change socks (what a simple, but great gift), and as we rested, we placed our wet socks on our chests and awoke with nice dry footwear to be held in reserve for the next change.

There was little similarity between our maps and the actual terrain. The ruggedness and stringent circumstances gave all the more fertile opportunities to be a "truth teller" and physical and spiritual encourager. For combat chaplains, I would encourage the frequent use of Psalms 46, 23, and 91 (He is our fortress and refuge) and the blessed Gospels. We held squad-sized (eight to ten soldiers) devotional and prayer services time after time in this tough area, and they were very well attended.

In my Pastor's Book, the 17th of May was a day of great thanksgiving! We returned from our supremely difficult mission. I can't over-emphasize the fact that it was of a super rugged and dangerous terrain, a prime place to be cut up by hostile fire. We had much to talk about, however—as "cliff climbers" and paratroopers of the mighty 173rd!

Also, 17 May was a significant day for me, as my mother was a daughter of Norway, and 17 May is Norwegian Independence Day, like our 4th of July.

Pentecost Sunday, 29 May 1966

On 29 May the text was St. John 14:23-31
Theme: "The Holy Spirit at Work—Now"
Hymns: "The Churches One Foundation," "Love Divine All Love Excelling," and "Now Thank We All Our God."

It was not unusual to have nearly a dozen worship services on a Sunday. If the companies were at a distance, we used a chopper to get to all of them. Even if some of our troops were on a search-and-destroy mission, services of worship were offered whenever the chaplain arrived. The services would not exceed one-half hour each. The Word and the Meal of Thanksgiving (holy communion) would be offered at each service.

Under hostile conditions, the worship was set up thusly: The Protestant Sky Soldiers would hold the perimeter and the Catholic troops would assemble for Mass. Then, the Catholic Sky Soldiers would hold the perimeter and the Protestants would fall into the center for worship.

THERE ARE NO ATHEISTS IN THE HEAT OF COMBAT

The Protestant prayer in that hostile place was generally, "Lord, raise up more Catholic Christians—for the perimeter."

We would have devotions from the book of Psalms for our dear Jewish Sky Soldiers. This was indeed a regular procedure in the field—on mission and in hostile territory. Rarely did a day go by that each chaplain in the 173rd did not have worship, Mass, devotional service, and prayer fellowship.

One dear and most trusted chaplain, Major (Fr.) Jim Kennedy, was forever on the line with our soldiers. He is a great shepherd/pastor/priest to all soldiers and dearly loved.

It is worthy of note that our precious Sky Soldiers had warm and giving hearts. They would forever give food—fruit, bread, rations, and candy—to children. If the youngsters had infirmities or sores, the soldiers would render medical help. They would always assist with basic needs as they moved on their missions. They loved and cared for children and families but always remained watchful and alert for potential danger as they helped the populace.

For the 12 June worship, the Scripture was I Peter 1:3-9: "Blessed be the God and Father of our Lord Jesus, who gave us a new and living hope, by the Resurrection of Jesus Christ, from the dead;"

Sermon theme: "Living Hope"

Hymns: "Living for Jesus" and "Stand up for Jesus."

The living hope theme and victory in Christ Jesus was wondrously heard and received. The soldiers grew in grace, meaning, and purpose. Indeed, spirituality was enhanced in a most life-changing and life-energizing way as the Word of God was honored and faithfully used.

On 13 June we went swimming in the South China Sea. This was most helpful for most of our soldiers— including ole "Ish" (myself). We had much bamboo poisoning on our bodies, particularly our hands, forearms, and necks had open sores. The salt water was an absolute cure. It was most helpful and fun filled. A strong alert was given to us, however: be careful, as the South China Sea has one of the highest populations of sharks. We were watchful!

On 14 June I had a grand meeting and visit with a dear friend, Master Sergeant Richard Bucholtz. We shared in holy communion together, shared in family information, and the fact that he gloried in receiving daily letters from his dear wife Barbara. (*JWW note:* Three decades later this patriot and wonderful friend of Connie's would lose a most loved daughter, seven months' pregnant—to the senseless and notorious bombing of the Murrah Federal Building in Oklahoma City.)

Our chaplains regularly flew to the hospital area where our wounded and / or injured troops were being cared for. The medical team did most excellent work in caring for our beloved soldiers. There were times as we visited our 173rd ABN soldiers that a large group of wounded soldiers were flown in for immediate care. Since we were familiar with hospital work and aid for soldiers, we would often be asked to pitch in and cut away clothing so that the medical team could get at the wounds quickly. This we would do while audibly praying the Lord's Prayer and the 23rd Psalm, as well as Psalm 46, John 3:16, and I Peter 1:3-5.

On 19 June, the extreme joy of receiving personal mail was nearly overcoming. It was Father's Day and a deep longing filled my heart for our three daughters and two sons (Beverly, Miriam, Gracia, Randy and Tim). This became a very special day. The children's greetings and messages of love arrived. My heart was filled to overflowing, and I wept tears of thanksgiving and joy.

Because of that emotional blessing of hearing from my family, when I had the opportunity to send home a message to the 173rd Sky Soldiers' families, we deeply encouraged the families to write letters to their loved ones. Indeed, we had churches send letters to the chaplain for distribution to soldiers—true kindness in action. It was thrilling! Most meaningful messages and pictures came from youngsters in the States, writing from their schools to the American soldiers. Usually, there was a connection—a 173rd Sky Soldier family member or friend in that school. Our troops thrilled in such life-encouraging letters.

On 23 June, without much fanfare, Operation Yorktown was launched. It was centered in Xuan Loc Province, approximately thirty-five miles east of Bien

Hoa—our home base. At first, the brigade met only sporadic resistance, but that was to change on 29 June. (*JWW note:* The events covered by the next few paragraphs could have—and perhaps should have—an entire booklet devoted to them.)

A Most Memorable Day—God Be With Us!

I was with "A" Company, 2/503rd Infantry on this mission. We became engaged with an enemy force 75 to 100 strong, and they were well dug in. The Viet Cong employed M-79 grenade launchers and 50-caliber machine guns on the Sky Soldiers. Heroism abounded as they overcame the VC.

Great soldier after great soldier did supreme acts of courage and heroism. A dozen of our beloved soldiers fell that day—to include one of my dear lay deacons—Acting Sergeant Fred Fritts.

Fred and all the soldiers of A Company had an enriching worship and holy communion service just prior to the operation. Acting Sergeant Fritts assisted me in communing our Sky Soldiers. He was a special person, and we visited many times in our months together. There was a natural "hook-in" in that he was from a clergy family. His father was one of our outstanding Episcopalian Army chaplains. I later wrote the dear family about carrying precious Fred's body off the battlefield.

Each soldier—ever so important, ever so valuable—fought with dedication and honor as a hero on that most difficult day of 29 June 1966 near Xuan Loc. (*JWW note:* I cannot find the words to express how difficult it was for Connie to relate the foregoing and the following to me.)

I arrived in the battle area with the relief troops. We did much damage to the VC, but we suffered exceedingly. I listened to stories of heroism as I visited each soldier. I had prayer and shared God's Word with each wounded soldier...and closed the eyes of the blessed dead. I rendered the laying-on of hands and used words of anointing for the sick and for each dear dead or wounded soldier. I spent time with each soldier encouraging and sustaining them.

The three growths of trees—small, medium and exceedingly large—caused us to work hard, very hard, to prepare an opening to get the wounded out. After considerable effort, and under serious sniper fire, it was achieved. The Air Force's Jolly Green Giant lifted out our beloved wounded, one-by-one.

Our bigger-than-life hero of the day—SSG Charlie Morris—would not allow himself to be lifted out until all of his wounded troops were first lifted out of harm's terrible way. SSG Charlie Morris was hit 33 times— several major wounds and many fragment wounds. (*JWW note:* As indicated in the Preface, Charlie Morris was awarded the Congressional Medal of Honor.)

SSG Charlie Morris's statement describes that day of 29 June 1966:
During the cutting of an evacuation LZ, we came under heavy sniper fire. Several trees prevented the evacuation of the wounded. The many wounded were lying near the trees and at the base of a large mound. The trees hung over and close by the mound.

As the men worked feverishly to prepare the LZ, the sniper fire continued to harass. Some of the men were so seriously wounded that they could not be moved, thus those blocking trees had to fall.

Under continued sniper fire, Chaplain Walker climbed the mound, the highest point, with a rope and he threw the rope around the tree. As the tree was being chopped, he stood in the most vulnerable spot, under fire, where he threw/pressed his body weight and strength against the tree to direct its falling away from the wounded.

He repeated this gallant act several times under heavy sniper fire with total disregard to his person and with evacuation of the wounded paramount in his actions. He then assisted in carrying each wounded man, including myself, to the litter hoist for evacuation. He brought hope and a desire to live to each wounded man. While he was assisting in carrying me, we came under heavy sniper fire. The chaplain never faltered. He just shouted, "Never mind that, we must get the wounded out!"

To make this gallant activity even more highly dangerous, the mound was littered with live dud grenades from the exceedingly heavy fighting. Yet, he pulled the trees as they were being chopped down into the host of dud grenades and walked among them loosening the rope and again climbing the mound under fire and retying to another tree and repeating the same action until the area was cleared to enable the evacuation of the wounded.

As each soldier was being prepared to be lifted out, I had prayer with them, mostly (again) the Lord's Prayer and the 23rd Psalm, John 3:16, and I Peter 1:3-5. Even though it was near dark, I crawled around the entire perimeter and made a pastoral call on each soldier for the "laying on of hands," prayer, and Scripture.

It was turning dark fast so we could only lift the wounded out. The dead stayed until morning. I slept among the dead to insure that they were indeed returned to their dear families: the moms and dads, wives, children, and grandparents. It was a night of near exhaustion but a night of deep and solemn prayer in our Lord's name. The chaplain was to be with his flock, wherever they went, and most assuredly when they were in the dark valley of death.

The following day I went around the perimeter and conducted a pastoral visit with each Sky Soldier. I held small groups of devotional services. It was unwise to assemble in a large group, as the area was still extremely dangerous with serious sniper fire.

The faith life of the soldiers grew immensely. This was a time of dynamic ministry. Many new names were written in the "Book of Life." Many came to a deeper and lasting faith. Our great Good Shepherd was there! (*JWW note:* For his Herculean effort on this operation, Connie was awarded the prestigious Silver Star.)

As I reflect on the period just discussed, I'm readily reminded of the outstanding leadership of Captain Jack Kelly and his First Sergeant Tony Torres during those most trying times. I studied God's Word and prayed with Jack Kelly, a most outstanding and caring leader/ soldier.

Jack was doing some deep personal wrestling about his life calling—to include full-time Gospel work. Jack, indeed, has gone on to great Christian leadership and is today one of our esteemed lay leaders, recruiters, and teachers in the Pentecostal fellowship. He and I did considerable reading in the book of Acts (our Lord's first New Testament history book), a deep mission-minded book for us at that time. (*JWW note:* Jack Kelley has shared with me a tape of the teaching seminar he conducts all over the country, called "Standing in the Gap," in which he uses Fred Fritts, Charlie Morris, and Connie Walker as heroic examples of God's workings in progress.)

July 1966 brought other operations: Aurora I, 9-17 July, and Aurora II, 17 July-3 August.

On 10 July 1966, the sermon text was I Peter 3:8-15; Sermon theme: "Reverence Christ as Lord"

Hymns: "Rock of Ages," "Oh God, our Help in Ages Past," and "Beautiful Savior."

The objectives of Operations Aurora I and II in north Long Khanh Province were primarily search and destroy and also to cut off Viet Cong tax-collecting activities in the area. Chaplains walked with and accompanied Sky Soldiers throughout, so that they would know that the Lord of Lords walked with them. Soldiers, therefore, knew that they were never alone—never abandoned. I divided my time as equally as I could from company to company to ensure seeing and being with as many troops as possible.

I was wounded during Aurora II. The combat medic did an excellent job in patching me up. I was able to remain with the heroic 173rd Sky Soldiers and complete our mission together. Praise God! (*JWW note:* This was only one of several wounds that Connie received during his year in Nam. Out of concern for family members at home, only one was reported, however, and recognized with the Purple Heart. This dear friend of the soldier missed very little time by being off of his feet [this by his own choosing].)

11 July was a Red Letter Day for the 173rd ABN Sky Soldiers. Dear Chaplain (Fr.) Charlie Watters arrived as one of our cherished priests! Praise God!

In War, as Elsewhere, the Difference
Between Sanity and Insanity is—Humor

Our 17 July worship was memorable: Text: Romans 6:3.

Gospel: Matthew 5:20-26

Theme: "Alive and Living with God"

Hymns: "Stand up for Jesus," "I Love to Tell the Story," and "Rise up, O Men of God."

A fine soldier had said to me, "Chaplain, if I come to chapel, the chapel will fall in." With further encouragement, he came. Our chapel that day was a squad tent. A large chopper came close in and indeed the tent collapsed and fell in, and that dear soldier yelled out, "See what I mean, Chaplain?" (Laughter and more laughter!) I assured him that we are not the good, but the forgiven, thanks be to God! He responded nicely and returned for every service of worship and prayer.

3 August was another banner day for the 173rd when Chaplain Bob Crick arrived to do magnificent Team Pastoral Ministry. (*JWW note:* Chaplain Bob Crick—like all the chaplains Connie refers to in this book and other writings—could and should have entire books written about them.)

On 5 August, I was assigned to brigade just as Chaplains Charlie Watters and Bob Crick came aboard and brought the highest caliber of pastoring possible to our beloved Sky Soldiers assigned to the 2nd/503rd.

I held my last service as the 2nd/503rd Airborne Battalion Chaplain and made the physical move to Brigade with LTC Chaplain (Fr.) Xavier J. Gigliello. He had arrived on 15 July as our new brigade chaplain. Chaplain Giggs (or "Jello" to the troops) was a tough, wonderful and most dedicated priest.

The Scripture was Titus 2:11 and following, St. John 16:4 and following, and Luke 16:1-19;

Theme: "Our Great God and Savior, Jesus Christ"

Hymns: "My God, How Wonderful Thou Art," "Children of the Heavenly Father," and the Doxology.

My thoughts about the 2nd/503rd: I was blessed to have pastored, walked in and with, the company of true greatness!

During 4 September worship, the Scripture was St. John 15.

Theme: "Real Life is to abide in the Lord"

Hymns: "Abide With Me," "Sweet Hour of Prayer," and "Living for Jesus."

14 September—Wow! Blessing upon blessing: Rest and recuperation (R & R) in Hawaii to be with precious and loved wife, Ann. Our time together was magnificent and meaningful, filled with love, dialogue par excellence, joy, and hope. We spent time speaking and praying deeply and wondrously about the fruit of a great love—our children. As the marvelous respite drew to a close, our great remembrance will always be the drama of the fun and the relief from the horror of combat.

26 September-9 October: Operation Sioux City. I stayed with the troops all the way through the mission, as was our pastoral practice.

10-17 October: Operation Robin. We lost four honored soldiers—two officers and two enlisted men—to Claymore mines while out on a mercy and care mission. I was invited to go with these dear soldiers on this mission. Just before departing, our S-1 (adjutant administrator) came out and advised me that we had a new artillery battery commander, a Captain Elliot. It was well known that I desired to make an immediate pastoral call/visit with each new commander. I disembarked

from the jeep and went to see Captain Elliot. The four
soldiers went on…and died. I am ever so thankful to be
called to be about our Father's urgent business.

I held continuous study groups and instruction
classes leading toward holy baptism, church membership, and confirmation any time we were not under
enemy contact. I met daily with troops concerning life
and faith matters, individually and in small groups. It
didn't matter what the troops' background might have
been, I would baptize by immersion or by pouring, as
appropriate to their heritage and background and covenant faith. Many new names were added to the Book of
Life, and many blessed Sky Soldiers came to know their
Heavenly Father and personal Savior, Jesus Christ!

On 30 October the Scripture was Hosea 13:1, Ephesians 6:10-17, Romans 1:16-17.

Theme: "God Turned on the Lights"

Hymns: "A Mighty Fortress is our God," "I Love to
Tell the Story," and "Come Thou Almighty King." There
were seven services this day along with hospital calls at
93rd EVAC and 3rd Surgical.

1 November: We had the officers' study group,
sponsored by Majors George McCoy and Dale Friend-
dear, dear comrades and heroes of the faith in our
beloved country.

6 November: I was called to II Field Forces area and
a visit from one of our senior pastors, Deputy Chief of
Chaplains Brigadier General Frank Sampson, later to
become our chief of chaplains (now at home with our
gracious Lord). Chaplain Frank Sampson was a valued
leader and a heroic man of God. There were six services,
all with the Lord's Supper.

On 27 November, the First Sunday in Advent (a
most wonderful beginning of the new church year), the

Scripture was Jeremiah 31:31-34, Romans 13:11-14, and Matthew 21:1-9.

Theme: "Get Ready!" (*JWW note:* As taken from Connie's series based on the Jump Commands.)

Hymns: "O Come, O Come Emmanuel," "Jesus Shall Reign," and a sing-along of the Sky Soldiers' favorites.

Then came boxing lessons at headquarters (held each week when not on special mission). The added blessing was always a fine cookout (generally a large steak) provided by our special friends—the cooks and mess sergeants. This day also was blessed with the fellowship of neighboring pastors—Chaplain John Staples, a pastor/counselor of the highest order, from the 3rd Surgical, and Ernie Wenzel, the dedicated chaplain of the engineers.

11 December: Our worship service came under sniper fire. Several soldiers left the service, returning a short time later. There was no further sniper fire!

19 December: One of our wonderful Sky Soldiers ran over an enemy mine, resulting in one blown-up truck. Praise God, the soldier was okay. The soldier was, however, covered with black powder and kept saying, "Man, what a bang!" He was also quick to advise all within hearing range, "I'm no foot soldier, I'm a wheel soldier." I was able to help him get another set of wheels.

On Christmas Day, 25 December, the Scripture was Isaiah 7:10-14, Titus 2:11-14, and St. Luke 2:1-14.

Theme: "Fear not! I bring you great joy"

Hymns: "Joy to the World," "Hark! The Herald Angels Sing," and "Silent Night."

There were worship services from early in the morning until late in the evening.

On 26 December, one of our sergeants accepted Christ as Lord! The wonder of the good news—the message of joy and peace in Christ Jesus—was faithfully heralded forth on those magnificent days of Christmas. Authentic meaning, hope, and joy were given and felt amidst the soldiers through St. John 1:1 and 1:14; "The Word was made flesh, and dwelt among us. We beheld His glory, glory as of the only Son of the Father."

1 January (1967): Happy New Year!

The message on 1 January was "Newness Par Excellence."

Hymns: "Come Thou Almighty King," "Beautiful Savior," and "Holy, Holy, Holy."

We made careful and pastoral hospital calls on our soldiers in the 3rd Surgical and 93rd Evac. Hospital, as well as on the whole medical staff and caregivers. The chaplain team would make regular hospital calls and make sure every soldier was visited by the pastor/chaplain.

Our continuous point of contact was our chaplain section NCOIC, Staff Sergeant Elwood Owens. He made sure that we knew when our soldiers were in the area hospitals. He was a top soldier/leader.

6 January: The Epiphany of our Lord Service.

Theme: "Wise people still come and worship him"

Hymn: "We Three Kings."

Following the service, I had a tremendous visit with dear friend Major Jerry Bethke (MG Retired). We shared many tales about family, the future, and most notably the living faith. He took great delight in sharing a story about his son with ole "Ish" (the boxing instructor), and how his son used (in self defense) one hand of lightning and the other of thunder.

5-25 January: Operation Cedar Falls. We received considerable sniper fire and some deadly Claymores.

15 January: From early until late, we had eleven services. I had chopper rides from place to place with

the last service and drop-off at 1910 hours in the 2/503rd area. It was very cold and I had no poncho. Oh, fond memories of Hawaii!

Amid all search-and-destroy missions, a sense of humor remained ever so sure and so sharp with our American soldiers. An example would be 21 January...

Lieutenant Strickler, who only seconds earlier had put on his helmet, was hit in the head when a Claymore blast ripped our area (and which went through the head gear). Strickler was knocked out and fell at the feet of Lieutenant Gus Vendetti, a valued friend. Gus thought that he was dead. Gus jumped up and asked the chopper pilots to quickly lift Strickler to the 3rd Surgical Hospital. They did so, and soon Strickler woke up.

As his friend's eyes opened, Gus said, "You have great jump boots. Will me your jump boots." There was deep and appreciative laughter all around the area. Tenseness (will my friend be okay?), then tenderness and thanksgiving (he is okay!)—thanks be to God! Solid friendships abounded and were full of zest. The American soldier appreciates humor and hilarity.

On 22 January the theme was Christian Growth and Leadership Training. On 26 January at 1000 hours, we had a memorial service at 3/503rd and at 1700 hours, a memorial service at 17th Cav. On 27 January was the study of God's Word with soldiers of all ranks and ages, Brigade chaplain's meeting and devotional services together.

1 February: Meeting with Church of God leadership from Cleveland, Tennessee. The general overseer was Rev. C. Raymond Spain, a deep man of God. We were blessed to have devotion from the Word of God and prayer together. I shared with him the courageous and brave information about Chaplain Robert Crick and

Brother Spain was elated to hear about Chaplain Crick's bold and winning ministry for our Lord Jesus.

On 19 February, 2nd Sunday in Lent, the text was St. Luke 9:51-56, II Corinthians 5:14 and following.

Theme: "The Cross and the Crown"

Hymns: "In the Cross of Christ I Glory," and "My Faith Looks Up To Thee." The same service was given for 17th Cavalry Brigade, headquarters, and the 2nd/503rd.

A Combat Jump

22 February: Operation Junction City. The 2nd/503rd Infantry Task Force spearheaded Operation Junction City by jumping into combat deep in war zone "C," near the Cambodian border. It was the first and only major American combat jump in Vietnam and the first anywhere since Korea.

The 1st and the 4th battalions came into adjacent landing zones by air/mobile assault. The objective was to locate and destroy the Central Office South Vietnam (COSVN), the supreme headquarters of the Viet Cong in the Republic of Vietnam. Within a short time, the 2nd Infantry of the 503rd Airborne Battalion, as well as artillery, and the central and support teams were ready for full-scale combat. The combat jump was a success!

Three chaplains made the jump from three different aircraft and in three different places in the jump stick. One chaplain was toward the front, one in the middle, and one near the end—pushing the stick. That way if an aircraft, for some reason, aborted, two chaplains would make it in with the troops. The placement also assured that the 173rd would have chaplain/pastoral coverage throughout the drop zone; one at each end of the DZ and one in the middle. The wise plan worked perfectly.

Chaplain pastoral coverage was complete throughout the drop zone.

Make no mistake; it was a combat jump—dropping the Airborne troops near the 700-foot level so that not too many shots could assail the Sky Soldiers on the way down.

Humor once again manifested itself. Coming close to landing with a parachute landing fall, I was audibly laughing as if I were having a good time. A tremendous young sergeant crawled over, asking, "Chaplain Walker, did I hear you laughing as we landed?" My smiling face answered, "Yes, indeed. The thought entered my mind that the VC had to be pretty poor shots to miss me!" (*JWW note:* Remember that Connie was a large lineman and a heavyweight boxer.)

He joined me with a quick laugh, then asked, "Don't you have a weapon?" I said, "Yes, son, I have the mighty Word of God and the Sacraments with me."

"Wow! Thank God for your trust in the Lord," he said, "but I'm telling you that I wouldn't be out here without a weapon and hand grenades." I blessed him and he was on his way as a bold and courageous leader.

I would have the world remember: Chaplain (LTC) Xavier J. Gigliello and Chaplain (Major) Fr. Charlie Watters. Three chaplains participated in the combat jump for Junction City, and only one is living this day. The two that are with the Heavenly Father were absolutely phenomenal pastors and priests with the most gallant of spirits—and a deep willingness to lay their lives on the line to help, save, and assist our beloved soldiers in their walk with the Lord.

And history records just that.

Chaplain Charlie Watters was awarded the Congressional Medal of Honor (posthumously), caring for, and ministering to soldiers at Dak To.

The Sky Soldiers would deeply feel the loss of our dear friend, Chaplain Gigliello, as he had fallen prey to wounds from a punji stick on one of our many river crossings. He would leave this earthly existence at Walter Reed Hospital (from other causes) several months after I returned to the States. I was honored to be with him at the time. God truly blessed all that knew him. Fellow priests were at his bedside, blessing, anointing and preparing him to meet our glorious Father face to face in heaven.

The day prior to the jump (21 February), we celebrated with the Word of God and holy communion together. I used, often, messages based on the Jump Commands and the Paratroopers' Prayer (see both elsewhere in this book). We had three marshaling worship services and private prayer with many Sky Soldiers who were deepened in faith and came to a living faith with our Lord Jesus for the first time. Two special messages were "Our Good Shepherd;" Scripture: St. John 10 ("I am the door"), and St. Luke 23:39-43; Theme: "Three Crosses, Representing All of Humanity."

All people—all soldiers—are represented here: Jesus in the center, one scoffing and insulting to the end, and one came to Jesus in faith and received the promise: "Today, you will be with me in Paradise." The response was most positive and heartening. Born anew and renewed relationships with our Lord, were grandly experienced.

Some of our "elite" soldiers were on escape and evasion from our Lord but marvelously and miraculously became dedicated and committed to our crucified and risen Lord Jesus. Thanks be to God! Human urgency and a sense of one needing help does indeed usher a person to and closer to the Lord, our Redeemer and Comforter.

The 173rd had been blessed with a group of exceedingly strong pastors/chaplains. They were physically strong and true spiritual giants. A fine example would be Billy T. Smith, a Cumberland Presbyterian, who the soldiers honored and loved. It was an awesome honor to work side by side with such phenomenal clergy persons from rich and diverse backgrounds; they were all captured by the mission of ministering to Sky Soldiers in any and all places and conditions, in the name of our great giver, God.

Special recognition should be given to my jump master on that historic day 22 February 1967. Major Jerry Bethke (MG Ret.) was and is a dear friend. I thankfully am able to visit, even to this day, he and his cherished wife, Phyl, in the San Antonio area. He is a great leader, commander, and servant of Christ Jesus.

2 March: My 35th birthday. On this date, I was awarded the Silver Star presented by General John Deane. I praise God to just be alive and pastoring soldiers. To God be the glory.

3 March: Heavy contact and fire fights on 3 March. Alpha and Charlie Companies were hard hit with many soldiers killed and wounded, and still the chaplain/shepherds were there with the dear soldiers.

On 12 March the Scripture was Numbers 13, John 3:14 and following.

Theme: "The Cross—The Way Home"

Hymns: "What a Friend We Have in Jesus" and "My Faith Looks up to Thee."

On 13 March we returned to home base, Bien Hoa, for a well-attended service of Thanksgiving. We had a cluster of commitments to the Lord and several baptisms. Notably, we had a luscious steak dinner of Thanksgiving with the troops.

26 March: Easter Day. The Resurrection of our Lord!
Scripture: Mark 16
Theme: "The Great Gospel Day"
Hymns: "Jesus Christ Is Risen Today," "Children of the Heavenly Father," and "Christ the Lord is Risen Today—Alleluia."

We had twelve services from early morn to late evening—and had four more on Easter Monday with a tremendous Resurrection response and bold action of love and faith with the Sky Soldiers throughout the command.

We visited all troops in the hospital. I was also able to visit with a dear mentor and friend (from 101st Airborne Ft. Benning days) in the II Field Forces Command, Chaplain (Col.) Holland Hope, a chaplain's chaplain, but mainly the soldiers' chaplain, also now in the bosom of our Lord.

2 April: First Sunday after Easter. Scripture: Proverbs 7:1-3, Mark 16;
Theme: "God's Word To Us—Jesus Christ Is Lord!"
Hymns: "Rise Up O' Men of God" and "What a Friend We Have in Jesus."

The Excitement—and the Blessings—Never End

On 2 April, I was ordered out of the jungle and combat zone just days prior to departure home to the States. An urgent call from 2/503rd came in for resupply, however, as they were in heavy contact with the enemy.

A chopper with ammunition and weapons was warming up. I quickly put on combat gear and armed with the Word and Sacrament, I climbed aboard. I just barely fit since supplies were stacked up to the ceiling of the chopper. We lifted off in prayerful attitude.

As we came near the 503rd area, we were shot out of the air! Our chopper pilot, WO1 Quiberg, took a nasty hit to the leg. First Lieutenant Tarr took the controls while we threw out ammo and supplies, preparing for a crash landing. We had lost hovering capabilities. Huge mahogany trees loomed everywhere, and we searched for an opening. Were those smaller trees and a creek bed? Yes! Thanks be to God, the small trees caught us and set us down rather gracefully.

Later the brigade surgeon told me that when the "May Day, May Day!" went out, Father Gigliello heard the call and in the midst of the brigade area cried out in prayer, "Lord, Lord, and Mother Mary, watch over my Lutheran friend, that he may go home to his family in the next days." Amen! The Lord did it.

VC were running all over the area. A relief party from the 2nd / 503rd came to our aid. They moved along to our position and policed up all the ammo and supplies as we quickly found our way to the perimeter. We carried the pilot to the battalion doctor for immediate medical care.

It was indeed a close call on one of my last days in country. The magnificent chaplain of God, Charlie Watters, and I quickly held Mass and a Service of Thanksgiving. At the beginning of the service, we had a nice attendance. Suddenly, airships appeared and, as gun ships, they started firing on the entire perimeter and beyond. We hit the ground. Wow! When we looked up to start the service again, the attendance had quickly grown by about fifty Sky Soldiers. We had a very well-received service of prayer, praise, and thanksgiving. Praise God!

An exciting and fulfilling day! The last day in the direct combat zone, I was ordered back to base to clear and prepare for the journey back home.

Wrap-Up!

To God be the glory and praise. We rejoice in the answered prayer in our Lord's name. I made hospital calls at the 93rd EVAC and the 3rd Surgical Hospital.

3 April: Briefed new troops—"Give the gift of trust and hope to fellow Sky Soldiers, in the Lord of trust and hope."

4 April: Prayer breakfast for the troops.

6 April: Baptized and confirmed Larry Smith. Thanks be to God! At 1700, I had dinner with Chaplain Ernest Wenzel, a true pastor of the faith. We joyously prayed together.

9 April: 0900—Worship at 3rd Surgical Hospital with Chaplain John Staples, a pastor par excellence; 1100-service for 2/503rd forward area.

10 April: Brief new troops on "Mission of Life in our Lord" and "Opportunities for Cherished, Deepening in your Faith and Prayer Life." At 0930—Awarded Army Commendation Medal (ARCOM) to assistant Ray Fredrich, a great troop and friend.

11 April: Memorial Service;

12 April: Depart for the flight home; and

19 April: Oh, Happy Day! Home!

Praise God! To Him be the Glory! Amen!

Attention to Order! (General Orders #584, 7 February 1967):

AWARD OF THE SILVER STAR

Walker, Conrad N. - Republic of Vietnam.

"For gallantry in action in connection with military operations involving conflict with an armed hostile force in the Republic of Vietnam: Major (then Captain) Walker distinguished himself by exceptionally valorous actions on 29 June, 1966 while serving as chaplain with a unit engaged with a large Viet Cong force near Xuan Loc. Chaplain Walker accompanied a relief platoon to the site of a vicious firefight where many men were dying or wounded. He ignored the hostile rounds striking all around him, to bring spiritual aid to the casualties. He also helped the medic to bring the wounded men back from the direct line of fire, despite the machine gun fire, which intermittently raked the area. When the Viet Cong were driven from the crucial positions, Chaplain Walker further exposed himself to incoming fire to prepare a landing zone for evacuation helicopters. He tied ropes onto the trees being chopped down and stood in vulnerable places, to pull the trees away from the wounded, as they fell. Without a thought of his own safety, he then carried wounded men to the aircraft. Throughout this firefight, Chaplain Walker gave no heed to the unexploded, but highly dangerous grenades littering the zone, or the deadly sniper fire. Major Walker's gallantry in action was in keeping with the highest traditions of the military service and reflects great credit upon himself, his unit, and the United States Army.

—By direction of the President—

CHAPTER 8

HOME AGAIN

Psalm 103:1-3. "Bless the Lord, my soul; my innermost heart, bless his holy name. Bless the Lord, my soul, and forget none of his benefits. He pardons all my guilt and heals all my suffering."-NEB

Mark 5:19. "Jesus . . . said to him, 'Go home to your own folk and tell them what the Lord in His mercy has done for you."-NEB

The absolute wonder and jubilance of it all—to be home with my loved family after a trying, difficult, and yet most rewarding adventure as a combat chaplain. Tears of joy were unashamedly celebrated in the warming and renewed presence of my loved spouse, Ann, and the fruit of our great love: Beverly, Miriam, Randy, Tim and Gracia. The joy was amplified by being with beloved parents, extended family and friends.

I was aware that the crescendos of the most profound and grace-filled elation and joy were nearly overcoming. Truly, it was a work of the Holy Spirit. It is He who calls us to deeper life in family and in faith in Christ Jesus. It is He who gathers us in His presence and in the presence of the friendly forces of love and grace. It is He who enlightens us in daily renewal and assurance of salvation and authentic Thanksgiving and joy without measure.

That was our experience of coming together as a redeemed family of God. Truly it was a foretaste of the gift of God at the heavenly banquet. Zest for life—his kind of life—is part of his revelation and his ever-present grace upon grace, in the realization of Matthew 22 and Mark 12: "Love the Lord your God with all your heart, soul, mind and strength, and your neighbor as yourself." Indeed, spouse, family, and friends are our closest neighbors. Truly, sobs have been turned into songs. To God be the honor and glory! Amen!

Fort Benning, Georgia: 1967-1969

Just prior to closing out the most eventful and cour-age-producing tour as combat chaplain with the 173rd, the chief of chaplains office advised me that our next mission/tour would be Fort Benning, Georgia, home of the U.S. Army Infantry and Airborne, Pathfinder and Ranger Schools. My mission would be pastor/chaplain to those very special and elite soldiers and their family members. It was an urgent mission in that as soon as these Airborne soldiers finished jump school, they would receive fifteen days leave and then most would be off for serious duty in combat.

This demanding, but fulfilling pastoral mission, was pregnant with great Gospel opportunities and care and keeping of our beloved soldiers that were of all ages and rank, diversified and rich backgrounds.

As I reported in to the post chaplain's office, Colonel Joe Andrews had changed things more to his liking and had assigned me to a historic and fine unit, the 197th Brigade at Kelly Hill. I had been in high expectation of serving the new and basic young paratroopers, Rangers and Pathfinders, but I knew that pastoral mission was pastoral mission—thus I saluted and reported to the 197th Brigade headquarters.

I had served only a few months when the new post chaplain, (Col.) Holland Hope, arrived—a fellow paratrooper, a world-famous marksman and a friend and mentor. He immediately moved me to the student brigade and the 4th Student Battalion that served the jump school, the Pathfinder school, and the Ranger school. The Ranger training took place in several areas: Camp Darby at Ft. Benning, north Georgia for the mountain phase, and north Florida for the swamp and jungle phase.

At that crucial time in our history, the Airborne school and department consisted of four weeks (now three) of tough, demanding training. The story that follows, after a closer look at jump school, took place shortly after I was assigned, and I found myself jumping five or six times a week.

The soldier, no matter what age or rank, is expected to report in for training at the prestigious Airborne school in top physical condition and with an eager attitude. The soldier must be ready to do the required push-ups, pull-ups, chin-ups, sit-ups and the four-mile Airborne shuffle consisting of one mile every seven and a half minutes.

A Look at Jump Training— and One Soldier's Experience

Jump school takes three weeks of very rigorous and intense training. The first week is called "Ground week," the second is "Tower week," and the third is "Jump week." Each week (training phase) is made up of one thousand troopers and is vitally meaningful and important in the future paratrooper's life.

Ground week is a run, run, run experience everywhere the soldier goes. The first challenge is to successfully execute a parachute landing fall (PLF), learning to hit the ground properly and safely. The PLF is done many times so that it becomes natural and even fun to do.

The next adventure is on the "swing landing trainer." This action assimilates an actual jump and PLF. The soldier, standing on a platform, puts on a harness that is attached to a rope that a noncommissioned officer controls. As the soldier jumps from the platform, swinging back and forth, the NCO releases the rope and the soldier executes a PLF. This action is done many times so that the soldier in the harness feels comfortable and proficient in this jump-assimilated action and contact with the ground.

This accomplished, the soldier moves on to the second week, or "Tower week," and the 34-foot tower. The tower has the soldier firmly and safely fit into a harness that is attached to strong nylon ropes, which in turn are attached to a cable. The soldier executes the 34-foot tower, sliding down the cable to a berm, unhooks, rushes back, climbs the tower again, and does it over and over until the soldier becomes proficient and the NCO says, "Okay, soldier, you are safe and ready to go on to the 250-foot tower."

The eager and ready soldier puts the past training into action as he, in a parachute, is lifted to the 250-foot level and dropped. This exercise negotiated safely, the soldier moves on to the very important last class of the week—the "Malfunction class."

The malfunction class instructs the soldier in all that can possibly go wrong with the parachute and how to correct it. The soldiers assemble on the training bleachers, and the NCO in charge clearly declares, "If you sit next to a soldier and his head is bobbing and eyes closing, give a sharp elbow in the ribs—this is a life-or-death class! Listen up! All must be alert and ready!"

As the class continues, a demonstration dummy is dropped from the 250-foot tower and smashes to the ground, since the canopy doesn't open (it's all part of the class). The NCO boldly declares a memorable piece of instruction, "When in doubt, execute the reserve parachute!" Another dummy is then dropped and the white canopy beautifully opens.

The third week of training is "Jump week." The best training in the world is ready to go into action. The first jump is usually from a C-130 or C-141 or the newer C-17. This is a time of deep thought and prayer. The aircraft flies in at 1,250 feet, giving an extra 250 feet of grace at the Airborne school; as a matter of information, all regular jumps are at 1,000 feet, even though a combat jump can be as low as 500 feet to prevent adversaries from having too many shots at the paratroopers on the way down.

Well, remember the malfunction class? Sure enough, one sleepy soldier had had his eyes closed, and his caring neighbor had given him a sharp elbow to the ribs. The soldier awakened and clearly heard the instruction, "When in doubt, execute the reserve parachute!"

On this particular day, the jump master gave the voice and hand signals as usual, "Get ready! Stand up! Hook-up! Check static lines! Check equipment! Sound off equipment check! Stand in the door! Go!"

It was a tremendous first jump for all—except one— the young soldier whose head had bobbed and eyes momentarily closed. As he exited the aircraft he thought, "Man, I'm in doubt!" Out came the white reserve parachute. He came down with two perfectly good parachutes! Meanwhile, he was thinking, "This is the end of time, the Parousia!"

When he landed, he did not have a good PLF. He came in flat-footed; he did not roll correctly; he landed on his buttocks; and because he did not tuck in his chin, his head flopped against the ground! The soldier was momentarily knocked unconscious and the white reserve canopy draped over him.

The Airborne school director, the command sergeant major, and I rushed over to the soldier. The soldier started to move under the white canopy with a case of the "big eyes." To him, this was the end of time.

After the jump, I still had on my headgear with a large Christian cross. I pulled the white canopy back, and the wide-eyed soldier asked, "Are you the Lord?" I quickly said "No, I'm one of his chaplains." The soldier only heard the word no! He loudly declared, "Holy smoke, I'm in real trouble!"

Immediately kneeling down and holding the soldier, I said, "You need not be in trouble because anything you might be afraid of our Lord handled on the cross and the resurrection, to include sin, death, and the evil one!"

He jubilantly and successfully finished his five qualifying jumps and became a full-fledged American paratrooper. Thanks be to God!

Those were days of considerable jumping, hence I received the tag of the "Leapin' Deacon." I generally jumped five times each week with the basic jump school troops—and I jumped at night with the Pathfinders and occasionally with the Rangers. The Ranger drop zones (DZs) were smaller and more rugged terrain—to include tree stumps. It definitely increased one's prayer life immensely (particularly the night jumps). This wondrous, close and direct soldier ministry mission was most blessed in the bearing of fruit and renewal.

Those years at the Airborne, Ranger and Pathfinder schools were pastorally productive and fruitful, beyond imagination and measure. There would be between one hundred and three hundred soldiers each week becoming new and renewed in the Christian faith. We would, of course, honor and amplify all faith groups, traditions, and faith lives. We were on a dynamic mission: to win, to hold, to develop, and disciple soldiers in the faith of our fathers—to bring soldiers to God and God to soldiers.

Our chaplain team was boldly and tenaciously up to the call—up to the gargantuan mission. Besides me, Chaplain (Fr.) Charlie Conroy (our tremendous Jesuit priest from Chicago, Illinois); Chaplain Robert Crick (Cleveland, Tennessee) and the unforgettable, heroic Chaplain David Heino (Minnesota and St. Louis, Missouri) made up the team. When we needed extra help, our great and beloved post chaplain, Holland Hope, would come and assist us in close pastoral and individual soldier-to-soldier ministry. We instructed in Holy Scripture, the catechism, the hymnal and special classes of instruction in preparation for holy baptism.

The supreme sense of urgency was captivating. Combat was immediately before most of these dear and dedicated young Americans. We baptized soldiers by the hundreds in the Airborne Chapel at Fort Benning. We also used the Chattahoochee River, just beyond the chapel.

As soldiers became new people in Christ and requested holy baptism and the instruction for holy baptism, we carefully sought to use the mode of holy baptism that was within the family faith and tradition. Each Friday evening, we would have a "river baptism," asking our new converts and newly renewed and instructed soldiers to come with two fellow Christian soldiers to witness their baptism in the Lord.

There was one young soldier (I shall ever remember) who, having made a commitment to Christ and desiring holy baptism, did not know how he wanted to be baptized for there were no godly or Christian parents. We then asked about grandparents who were people of faith. "Oh, yes! My grandmother is a Christian, and she's in fact called a Holy Roller."

That's all the information we needed. We knew how he was to be baptized. He returned on Friday evening with two Christian witnesses: one a Pentecostal Christian and one a Roman Catholic Christian, and down to the river we went. In fact, there were two truckloads of soldiers that were on hand that night—one for the newly committed and one for their witnesses and sponsors.

After all the baptizing was done, the two witnesses for the new Pentecostal were spotted on the bank, the one raising his arms in praise saying, "Thank you, Jesus! Thank You, Jesus!" The young Roman Catholic meanwhile, blessedly and quietly crossed himself, and prayed for his friend becoming a new person in Christ Jesus!

My instructions to my wonderful assistants were always the same, "Be vigilant for activity from any of the many water moccasins that called the river home. We don't want to lose a blessed soldier, and we definitely don't want to lose the chaplain." The foregoing tale is only one of many hundreds that took place during those grand, demanding, and exceedingly spiritually-productive years at Fort Benning, Georgia.

Along with all the pastoral work with the troops at Fort Benning, there was another most important and careful mission to perform and to prayerfully carry out—death notifications.

Fort Benning was not only the nerve center for the Airborne, Ranger and Pathfinder community; it was also the home of the U.S. Army Infantry. In front of the school stands the famous leadership statue depicting the combat infantry leader, with the powerful words, "Follow Me." Most impressive! It is also a serious indicator that casualties will take place in combat, and indeed they did.

Following some crucial battles in Vietnam, the Killed-in-Action (KIA) reporting and notification to American homes became vast. With such heavy casualties, the chaplain team was deeply involved with adjutant general personnel, medics, and a physician's nurse/caregiver. This need and action at certain times had the notification teams working from very early to very late.

Some American families received the news with deep grief, pain, and hurt. Generally, after a time of thought, prayer, and deep breathing, they would come to the painful realization that the notification team, as difficult as the missions were, was indeed "friendly forces" of care and support.

Some families reacted with attitudes of profound anger, disbelief, and hurt. They would often be in a state of shock, and at times they would strike out and physically attack—rare, but it happened. (At those times, it was most beneficial to have notification teammates with you.)

We tried in every way to follow through with another contact, a phone call or visit. This seemed to be most helpful for the family to have a personal contact, especially with a concerned and caring chaplain. The same chaplain would often be requested to conduct the military funeral. Survival assistance officers and NCOs were of great and amazing support and would often request the chaplain who had pastoral relationships with the family—due to notification—or through the Airborne Department.

All during the conflict, the infantry lost many blessed soldiers as they entered into combat with a dedicated unit, often an Airborne unit. The requests for an Airborne chaplain to conduct the funeral service for a Sky Soldier were heartbreakingly too frequent.

This difficult pastoral work was done along with one's own unit's work and most particularly with early morning four-mile-runs, sit-ups, pull-ups, chin-ups and push-ups. The military mission of the chaplain at Fort Benning was urgent, demanding, crucial, and most blessedly rewarding.

Along with all of these critical ministries, however, our family continued to celebrate and experience family night together—a fun time par excellence!

Along with home fellowship, activities at school, Sunday school, and scouts, we had a favorite family place that we visited on a monthly basis—Callaway Gardens, not too far from Fort Benning. We would depart early in the morning for a surprise trip. A hearty outing would start with a waffle and eggs, or pancakes and bacon, or oatmeal and toast and fruit—oh, my! We would arrive at Callaway Gardens and enjoy long walks, bike rental and riding—often walking the wonderful flower paths, where the aromas were a delight. We generally, usually, well, most of the time, had a most tasty and charming picnic lunch, and on special occasions, a cookout delight.

This was a period of joyous memory building. Callaway Gardens was our family retreat center. To this very day, our now-grown family members return for glorious periods of remembering.

A Good Respite!

One beautiful spring day, as I worked at the Airborne Chapel, two large, late model vehicles pulled up. Eight nicely dressed villagers (Lutheran lay leaders from Plains, Georgia) came forward and said, "We want to talk to the Lutheran chaplain, goes by the name of Connie Walker."

I stepped forward and shook their hands in a hardy way—they were strong in body and firm in the faith. They came quickly to the point. "We need help," the spokesman said. "We lost our pastor. Will you come and help us?" I felt moved by their strong and dedicated Christian spirits and their leadership.

I quickly advised them that I had services on Saturday evening, three on Sunday mornings and one on Sunday evening. "That is great!" they responded, "Soldiers and families should be first." They, however, pressed with, "How about serving us on Wednesday evenings—for a spell."

I was very impressed with their zeal, and checked with my post chaplain (Holland Hope), and he gave his blessing. So for the better part of a year, until they got another pastor, I served St. Andrews Lutheran Church in Plains, Georgia. St. Andrews, by the way, is very near former President Jimmy Carter's Baptist church. This was a fine experience and change of pace for our family, who frequently went along on Wednesday evenings— in fact; it became their Sunday—for a spell.

Once again, Humor is Always Present —if We're Open to it!

A dear and trusted friend, Chaplain Emil Dinkel, was alerted for duty in Vietnam.

Before he departed Fort Benning, he asked Ann and myself to carefully look after his wonderful wife, Mary Lou, and his two daughters and two sons. We joyfully watched over them as he requested. Our main mission, however, was to stay out of their way, as they were very strong, leader-type people. We remained close by and yet in the background.

Early in his Vietnam tour, a close family member died, and he returned to the States for the funeral. Emil stayed for a couple of weeks, during which time Mary Lou became pregnant. When she started to show a bit, Emil wrote from Vietnam, "Connie, watch after Mary Lou as you would Ann." Ann and I did so.

We spent time with their family, assisting as much as they desired. Emil again wrote, "Connie, Mary Lou is great with child. Do be most mindful and be with her as you would be with Ann, getting her to the hospital, etc." One day Mary Lou called and said, "It's time." Ann and I drove the mile and a half only to find that a neighbor had already taken her to Martin Army Hospital.

We rushed to the hospital, and I hurried into the labor room. As I held Mary Lou's hand and prayed with her, a matronly nurse came in and said, "What are you doing here?" I said that I was standing in for a friend who was in Vietnam. Shortly thereafter, Mary Lou delivered a healthy and active son—named Timothy John.

Emil sent a special message from Vietnam and a check for fifty dollars. "Connie, I give Mary Lou one dozen yellow roses for each child whenever another appears. Please do that for me—deliver the five dozen yellow roses."

I checked everywhere for the flowers. I went to the Post Exchange, but I received a big "sorry." I went to every florist in Columbus, Georgia—again, "sorry." Finally, one florist, as a patriot, took pity and called around an ever-widening circle. Voila! He found five dozen yellow roses in Birmingham, Alabama—but fifty dollars? I was told, "Get real!"

I got on the phone and spoke to the blessed, patriotic folks in Birmingham. They finally relented when I told them part of the story and that the soldier chaplain was on duty in Vietnam. "Okay! But how do we get them to you?" I told them that they should use the next Greyhound bus departing Birmingham, Alabama, and going to Columbus, Georgia, to transport the flowers. I sent them the fifty dollars and money for transporting the flowers.

Thankfully, Ann and I were able to deliver the five dozen yellow roses to Mary Lou's room. Ann went to the waiting room and who should come by but the matronly nurse (who didn't trust me anyway). With a pontificating spirit, she said, "I suppose you are standing in for your friend with all those yellow roses." I said gently, "Yes, ma'am, I am." She looked at the card attached to the patient's bed, looked at my name tag, and huffily left the room—breathing oaths as she departed. The cherished wife of Chaplain Emil Dinkel had great joy and tears in her eyes as she held her five dozen yellow roses. Praise God!

Remembrance of a Truly Inspirational Giant

I should be sorrowfully remiss if I did not share at least a small bit of publication space with the memory of a person who had a profound impact on the shaping of my military ministry and the U.S. Army chaplaincy.

While at Fort Benning, I was reunited with the late, great Chaplain (Col.) Gynther Storaasli, chaplain and mentor. His mentoring and leadership first blessed me during the years of my attendance at Luther Seminary and the early days of my National Guard involvement.

It is not possible to do justice to this remarkable gentleman's military accomplishments in the few words here devoted. Instead allow me to merely give a menu of his years here on earth.

Born 17 May, 1885 (Norwegian Independence Day)

Missionary to China—1914-1915

Parish Pastor—1915-1917

WWI Camp Pastor—1917-1918

Chaplain U.S. Army—1918-1948

Bureau of Service to Military Personnel, NLC—1948-1954

Director, Military Chaplain Commission, ELC—1954-1966

He authored a small but powerful book named *The Call*.

Among his many accomplished assignments were Chaplain School Commandant and notably the last Army Air Corps Chief of Chaplains. (*JWW note:* The very next day, his deputy became the first Air Force Chief of Chaplains and was promoted to the rank of Two Star General.)

Chaplain Storaasli retired in Columbus, Georgia. I was blessed to be his and Mrs. Sylvia Storaasli's pastor from 1967 to 1969. He, by the way, critiqued my sermons each week. He was a dear friend and an encourager—a true giant of the chaplaincy. Praise God!

CHAPTER 9

U.S. ARMY CHAPLAINS SCHOOL— FORT HAMILTON, NEW YORK

Psalm 27:1, 3-4. "The Lord is my light and my salvation; whom should I fear? The Lord is the refuge of my life; of whom then should I go in dread? If an army should encamp against me, my heart would feel no fear ... One thing I ask of the Lord ... that I may be constant in the house of the Lord, all the days of my life ..."-NEB

Mark 1:35-36. "Very early next morning he got up and went out. He went away to a lonely spot and remained there in prayer."-NEB

The Verrazano Narrows Bridge spanning the New York Harbor from Fort Wadsworth, Staten Island, to Fort Hamilton, Brooklyn, represents a passage from the Old World to the New World for many immigrants. So, too, does this short period of time represent a bridge between Connie's formative years in the Army and those of greater command responsibility.

Past are the days of hundreds of jumps with the troops, the frightening glories of war, and the comforting feeling of just being one of the guys. Instead, Connie found himself preparing for that most horrendous arena of duty the military "foists" upon a chosen few, Command Assignments at the U.S. Army Chaplains School. (*JWW note:* I'll let Connie tell the tale from here.)

Life in the big, bustling city of New York took the collective Walker family a bit by surprise and caused one to blink, since I'd just come from the super enthusiastic, demanding, and high-spirited Airborne Pathfinder and Ranger schools as chaplain/pastor. Suddenly we found ourselves not only in a new arena but the New York City arena!

At Fort Benning, we had a ranch type, comfortable home built for larger families. At Fort Hamilton, we were given a cigar box-sized apartment for a family of seven! We made it work!

At this historic time, the robust and hostile Vietnam demonstrators were regularly at our entrance gate carrying nasty signs and slogans and spitting as you passed by. It took real solid adjustments for our strong family to "hangeth in there" and do the best that we could under the conditions at that time. It deepened our reliance on our great God, Savior and friend and one another.

We took inspiration from the huge, majestic, and distinctive Verrazano Bridge. The witness of the bridge taught us something very important—that we are to be bridge builders to help and to enhance peoples' lives and not to build barriers and walls to hurt and hinder. This message went deep into our hearts as a caring and shepherding family.

A Verrazano Bridge Story

Chaplain (Fr.) John Kowsky, one of the Army's great and caring priests, was giving a class on being a "post chaplain." Suddenly a New York City police officer broke into our class and said, "Father, come quickly!

A teenaged male is climbing the Verrazano Bridge and is going to jump to his death." Father John's brother was a leader in the NYPD, so Father John himself was well known by the New York police force.

Father John paused at the door and said to our class, "On your knees and pray for this person!" The police took Father John to the place where the distressed youth had already climbed up part of the way. Father John climbed up to a place where he could be heard and spoke nicely and in a nurturing way to the potential jumper.

The teenager responded, and Father John could tell at once that he was a Brooklyn lad. This hard-nosed chaplain knew exactly how to handle this kid from Brooklyn. "You get your ass down here right now or I'll really clobber you!" The lad answered, "Yes, Fadder, I'm coming down." He did. Father John had ministered to him in a highly effective way.

The police brought our instructor back to the classroom. Father John came into the room saying, "Off your knees! The Lord did a miracle in saving this disturbed young person." This memory is a pastoral delight and gift from our U.S. Army Chaplain School—and a faithful chaplain and priest.

The Effect of the Assignment on the Family

Indeed, 1969-1970 was a most difficult, challenging, and growing year for the Walker family. The dear children, however, demonstrated a magnificent resiliency and positive learning ability in the New York school system (their first and only experience at an institute of learning with bars on the windows).

I served a parish in the Brooklyn area, Salem Lutheran, for the entire academic year as pastor and friend.

The congregation had a dynamic classical music and choir program. They had highly trained voices and did a masterful job, especially on Bach pieces. I specifically remember the grand organ with a tremendous organist, which added so much majesty and magnificence to the worship service while celebrating the mighty resurrection of our Lord Jesus. Praise God!

I taught confirmation classes, called on parishioners in hospitals and in some homes, and trained lay leaders in mission and outreach to be truth tellers on the line, at work, and within their changing neighborhoods.

The year's high watermark was the deepening of friendships and relationships with fellow chaplains and chaplain's assistants (along with the superb staff and chaplain school instructors). My advisor during the academic year was a bright and godly chaplain, Del Gremmels, a former missionary in Asia. Other highly valued experiences were the splendid speakers brought in such as the Army Chief of Staff, other senior leaders, and also resource professionals from the outside.

As challenging as this year was on the family, there were many, many upside moments, and high on the list was the food. Wow! New York pizza was prima, along with the very best Chinese offerings. Top-of-the-mountain baking was done by the Swedish ladies at Salem Lutheran, the pastries and breads were enjoyed after the worship and Sunday school services. The children remember that to this day. (*JWW note:* A general comment from the Walker family, "Boy, do the Swedish people know how to bake!")

We took advantage of invites and offers by kind friends. Sergeant Major Ted Arthur was at West Point (remember his story about the Army/Navy football game?), and we visited him and his family in their fine home area. We were invited to "come aboard" the

Academy superintendent's fine river vessel for tours and cookouts, always with Ted as host, often in association with his fellow sergeants major and their dear families.

I've got to mention again, those tickets were on the fifty-yard line! (*JWW note:* I'll finish up this short, but important chapter.)

There were other diversions for the family during this year of course, including sight-seeing (like any other tourist). The Big Apple is awesome for any first-time visitor and the Walkers were no exception. The museums, statues, parks, athletic events (hockey, basketball and baseball), the huge buildings, the Broadway shows, and concerts were all wonderfully memorable.

Though the year was tough on the family, otherwise, it increased their capacity to suffer and excel at the same time. There was school for the youngsters, ministry for Connie, shopping for Ann, and a springboard for future assignments that would carry much more responsibility, the military being what it is.

Thailand was to be the next adventure in this storied career!

CHAPTER 10

FAMILY LIFE

Proverbs 11:3. "Honesty is a guide to the upright, but rogues are balked by their own perversity."-NEB

Ephesians 1:2-3. "Grace to you and peace from God our father and Lord Jesus Christ. Praise be to the God and Father of our Lord Jesus Christ who has bestowed on us in Christ every spiritual blessing in the heavenly realms."-NEB

The tour in Thailand was an absolute delight for our whole family as they became adjusted and acclimated to the vast cultural shock and the peculiar lifestyles and experiences.

We kept just missing good housing opportunities. The first month and a half was spent in the Imperial Hotel, for it took nearly two months to get one's household belongings sent by ship, and you would start looking seriously after a month-plus in country. The Imperial Hotel was grand and colloquial living. Friendships developed for each family member.

The home that we finally secured belonged to the Lord Mayor of Bangkok, a fine villa. All military families had to live on the economy. We settled in on Soi

(Street) 55, but unknown to us at first was that our street had a nickname—the "Snake Street." We soon discovered why the nickname was assigned.

During our time in those beautiful and spacious quarters, the body count of very poisonous, deadly snakes rose to twenty-four. With the assistance of our gardener, Chun, we killed cobras (king and India), bamboo vipers, russell vipers, banded kraits (kin to the coral snake—but these dandies are four footers) and the deadly mamba.

All five children attended the International Bangkok School System—with pristine educators. The youngsters had to have a very early start each morning, 0430 hours. The early start and an early finish were necessary, since there was no air-conditioning and the climate was hot and humid. It was a tremendous blessing to have our children's education paid for, as it was very expensive for the non-military families. They were bused to school in the early morning (one-hour trip), and school began at 0600 hours.

The Thai people did very early morning shopping in their markets, which was a sight to behold and participate in. Ann sent Panum, her housemaid and helper, to shop and Chun, our yardman, for yard and home supplies. They became part of the family while we served in Thailand and were faithful and cared deeply for our children. The children wonderfully cared for and respected these special people.

Scouting was a big adventure in Thailand for our boys. Randy and Tim would go out on a scout camping adventure (we would also ensure that several Special Forces soldiers went with them), and as they departed, we would pray and bless them and then say, "Be careful of wild elephants, tigers, and cobra snakes, but other than that, have a great camp out."

It was a rich and dynamic experience to hike over fifty miles with all of the scouts to the bridge on the River Kwai. We stopped at each cemetery for a memorial service. The scouts were full of zest and life, but they noticed old vets from many countries who had served and had many, many friends die, show their pain by crying in remembrance.

Randy and Tim also participated in organized baseball, and they were fortunate enough to win the citywide Bangkok championship. They were sponsored by KLM Airlines, which forever gave them fine meals, picnics and gifts, and they learned and played some great baseball.

Our daughters, Bev, Miriam, and Gracia were deeply involved with our youth fellowship at the chapel and school happenings and events. They displayed and further developed great reading skills. We did not have a TV; consequently, reading became all the more deep and abiding in interest and practice. They had challenging and fun events along with their excellent study and devotionals.

Church Life

All the family was seriously and jubilantly involved in our monthly well-attended chapel family dining program and other fun events at one of the classical Bangkok hotels that we contracted from time to time. It was a grand joint event for the Catholic and Protestant communities. The banquets were of the highest and most attractive presentations. The considerable leftovers went to the homes of our younger soldiers' families. This was a fine boost for some who lived in a rather careful and austere manner.

The authentic friendship and fellowships experienced at these events in first-rate hotels, paid for by the chapel as an official monthly event, were supremely successful and service oriented. Our youth would perform skits, have singing groups, and dramatic readings and portrayals. Families and single soldiers had wonderful celebrations of life together—warm and caring relationships.

This chapel event grew in importance. We had an evening devotion and evening prayers and a visiting speaker. We were honored with the presence of the Chief of Chaplains MG Frank Sampson and world-class scholars like Dr. Oswald Hoffmann of the "Lutheran Hour," or a great athlete, and at times, a Soldier of the Month or of the Quarter as our special guest.

The splendid tour in Thailand gave us some dear and lifelong friends—Don Troyer and his lovely wife Nancy. Don was our senior chaplain's assistant. We were endowed with a cluster of gifted and caring chaplains' assistants. Don and Nancy were exceedingly talented vocalists and musicians and with their music brought many souls into a personal relationship to our Lord. Don went on to become one of our very best pastors and chaplains (until retirement from the Army), and they are still treasured leaders in their beloved Adventist Church.

A magnificent and loving group of Catholic nuns—the Sisters of the Good Shepherd—became regular visitors and participants in our community. The sisters operated a caring and helping facility for Thai unwed mothers—abandoned young ladies with child. As our friendship and trust grew, they made children available to American couples for adoption. Through God's grace, we assisted in placing many dozens of these precious little ones in American families who deeply and strongly desired a child or children.

The sisters taught the young Thai girls a vocation while with them: they made blankets, tablecloths, towels, sheets, placemats, dresses, and the like for sale. The sisters also taught basic office work, as well as cooking to aid them in employment and home life. This proved to be a rich relationship, and it wondrously blessed many American families and our Thai friends.

The soldier and family ministry in Thailand was an ever growing and expanding work. It was not an easy ministry, but it became very fruitful and meaningful. Soldiers respond to authentic and meaningful relationships and care. They forever came for counsel, study and a place to have a cup of coffee, Danish rolls, a coke, cookies, or a cool glass of safe and energizing water. The chapel was a place of care, trust, vision building and hope producing along with new and growing gospel life.

One of our highly-motivated soldiers fell in love with a gorgeous Thai young lady but unfortunately, she spurned his interest and advances. He was so hurt and disappointed that he climbed to the very top of the soldiers quarters—the Prince Hotel (six stories high). He jumped off and crashed into a cushioned van. He was rushed to the U.S. Medical Center in Bangkok. I, too, rushed to the emergency room as I was called by the 1st Sgt.

Miraculously, no bones were broken and no cuts. There were bruises and one front tooth chipped. I pastored to him and gave him a desire for living and hope in the Lord. I then suggested, "Soldier, you are tough and ready. Why not sign up for Airborne training?" He did so and grew in wisdom in his courting of young women relationships—among other things!

The Thai young ladies were a big and steady attraction to our soldiers. Many wanted marriage, and we responded with careful and challenging counsel and instruction. We provided English classes at the chapel, and we had local missionaries and educators come in and instruct on cooking so as to assure that our beloved soldiers had proper nourishment. We provided Thai wives a culture course run by Mrs. Maxine Stewart, a great instructor in English. She spoke fluent Thai, so this equipped her to do wonderful educational things in their lives.

The Thai Wives Course was open to any Thai wife or fiancé of any American on official assignment with the U.S. government. The classes were well attended and assisted our soldiers greatly. We were assured that our soldiers were eating properly and at the same time preparing the Thai bride to enter a new life in America.

The Thai wives called us (along with the kind and caring Sisters of the Good Shepherd) the "Christian Monks." Buddhist monks in orange garb were a regular experience in their lives, and they complimented us with their chosen name. Authentic care and love is caught, and the same is true with the faith life in our Lord—it is caught as well as taught. Indeed we were asked to provide Christian instruction and preparation for holy baptism for many requesting Thai wives and soldiers.

There's More to Thailand than Bangkok!

During this tour as chaplain to the USARSUPTHAI—and my area, specifically the Bangkok area, soldiers and families and the chapel center, I was also serving our 46th Special Forces troops in the Lopburi. I would spend most of a week at a time in their area visiting soldiers, having worship service and study groups, and I would spend evenings dining with soldiers and having prolonged visits, fielding any and all of their concerns and hopes. I would even jump with them periodically upon request, or go on a training exercise with them in their AO (area of operation).

These vigorous and strong soldiers liked to have meaningful and strong discussions, so we dealt with them and their concerns and faith matters where they were.

It was not unusual for the Green Berets to come visit and worship at the Bangkok Chapel and participate in our chapel family life.

During this important and historic tour of duty, we were inspired and encouraged by one of our Lord's special agents of grace in Command Chaplain Stan McMaster.

A Tale of Intrigue, Fit for the Tabloids

One of my early-on friends in Thailand ran the taxicab business near the Prince Hotel—our soldier's quarters/billets. I first met him as I regularly called on the troops staying in the Prince Hotel. I gave the taxi owner a "high" greeting with hands folded as in prayer and high on my chest. He quickly said that is too high and big of a greeting for an ordinary person. I said that this is the way Christian people greet others, for we hold all in high esteem. He smiled and let it pass.

My greetings were always the same to him. We drank hot tea together and visited and became friends. Although he almost always wanted to add a bit of rum to the tea, I explained that soldiers could not do so while on duty, and he always understood. This friendship took on special meaning as the tale continues.

Soldiers and their Thai wives took dedicated ministry, care, and time. One particular counseling session became dangerous, in fact, *exceedingly* dangerous, nearly costing Chaplain (Fr.) Neal Kelly and me our very lives.

Father Kelly was counseling one of his Catholic sergeants and his attractive wife. The counseling became intimate in husband and wife relationships. Father Kelly came to my office and briefed me and asked if I would kindly assist. I did so. The Thai wife came to an angry conclusion that Father Kelly and I were tilting in favor of our young sergeant, even though we were careful in keeping the situation even and level. I brought in Mr. Swake, our Thai male secretary and translator, to help us keep a careful and clear balance.

The Thai wife (who had many contacts in the criminal world) exploded in anger and jumped up and moved toward the door. Mr. Swake said, "Do not let her leave. She's dangerous like a Dragon Lady." We kept talking, trying to return to the counseling area. She vigorously pushed her way out of the door and said, "Christian monks, you are in deep trouble!" She was right. She put a "hit" on Chaplain Kelly and me—which of course meant that she hired killers to do us in!

My taxicab owner and friend immediately found out about the hit and called the chapel and said, "Christian monk, friend, get out of town quickly!" He said we would hear from him when all was okay. I called the Bangkok area commander and told him what was happening. He inquired, "Who told you about the hit?" When I told him my source, he said, "Wow! He is the Al Capone of Thailand. Do as he says." I told him that we were heading for the Special Forces camp in Lopburi.

As we pulled out of the chapel parking lot, two armed hit men with silencer-type weapons came in the parking area on a motorcycle. They charged into the chapel and into our offices looking for Chaplain Kelly and me. Our good man, Mr. Swake, told them that we had headed south toward the coast and the recreation area in Pattaya. We were safe far to the north in the Special Forces camp. After a couple of days, I received a phone call from our taxi owner friend saying, "Christian monks, my friends, all is okay. You come home now!" We did!

As soon as we arrived in Bangkok, I went to see my kind and life-saving friend. I gave him an extra high greeting. He smiled, and we had tea together—this time with rum. I asked him what had happened. He laughed, and then turning a bit serious said, "I don't ask you about Christian monk business, so don't ask me about my business." We laughed and understood each other. My friend then said, "The sergeant and his wife will be at the chapel at 0900."

Indeed, the next morning they were there. She was a bit roughed up but very much okay and with a big smile on her face. Later, as the relationship developed, the beautiful Thai wife and her sergeant husband received instruction and on the next Easter morning, she became a new—and he a renewed—Catholic Christian.

Lessons are many, but for sure it teaches us to honor all people, no matter their station in life. Love them in the name of our Lord. This actual happening was a profound gift to Chaplain Kelly and me. It deeply enriched our grace-filled prayer lives!

A Most Special Commander—and Friend

My senior commander of USARSUPTHAI was the great and legendary BG John Vessey, a true leader and Christian champion and friend.

Our relationship with BG (Jack) Vessey and his lady Avis and sons and daughter grew in deep friendship, trust, and admiration. He is a leader without peer. He and Avis have a wondrous and broad-gauged, bold, tenacious, and loving Christian faith and witness. We had some deep and mutual foundations as confessional Lutheran Christians and roots in the great state of Minnesota, where both of my dear brothers yet live, celebrate life, and remain dynamic leaders.

Each visit to Minnesota means a visit to the home of General Jack and Avis Vessey. We remain close and also have the delight of fishing together—with fine success.

The soldiers were blessed and filled with hope and trust as they saw the general visiting them and breaking bread together. He always was most interested in "Rear Row Rudy," (referring to the young and impressive soldier). The soldier had a friend and caring leader in General Jack.

And finally . . .

The pastoral mission in Thailand was most splendid. We saw blessed results of our labors of love in the Gospel, and yes, many new soldiers and family members made lifelong commitments to the Lord. Thanks be to the giver of life, the Holy Spirit.

CHAPTER 11

THE OLDEST ACTIVE ARMY POST WEST OF THE MISSISSIPPI

Proverbs 7:1-3. "My son, keep my words, store up my commands in your mind. Keep my commands if you would live, and treasure my teaching as the apple of your eye. . . . Write them on the tablet of your memory."-NEB

II Corinthians 13:5. "Examine yourselves: are you living the life of faith? Put yourselves to the test."-NEB

During the last months in Thailand, the list for Command and General Staff College at Ft. Leavenworth, Kansas, was announced, and my name was on it. Kansas was to become our new home for a year. We were thrilled, but it proved a mixed experience—joy and sadness.

Our eldest daughter, Beverly, had a few hours to take as a high school senior. She was nearly ready to graduate before we left Thailand (and the International School of Bangkok), but we discovered the refined truth a bit late to react. (*JWW note:* Seems like a familiar road taken by Connie in his college days.)

The classes that she desired were all filled in Leavenworth. The family tried hard to correct the situation, but the high school staff was not a friendly force. She then endeavored to take a lighter load, since she was nearly a graduate, and work to set aside funds for college or university. The high school, however, remained unfriendly and would not allow it (we discovered later that part of their motivation was federal funds for each student). Beverly nonetheless hung in and did an excellent job, again proving to be a most kind and caring person and leader in her own way.

Our second daughter Miriam attended junior high at Ft. Leavenworth and thus things worked nicely for her—again as a superior student and leader, full of zip and fun!

The three youngest had a most creative, splendid, and spiritually rewarding year at St. Paul Lutheran School. St. Paul Parish and Pastor Vic Pally were very kind to us as a family. Randy, Tim, and Gracia did very well during that year at St. Paul, a true blessing. They were full of life, spark, fun, and creative zest and eager to also grow in grace, holiness and wisdom at this marvelous school. Randy was confirmed in his faith and the affirmation of his baptism, a time of great meaning, assurance, and joy.

Command and General Staff College was a challenge and a time of enjoyment. This year was a true change of pace. There was a host of new friends, new opportunities, and a vast amount of reading. There were excellent lectures and guest speakers, and my classmates/sections were full of life, work, gaiety, and adventure.

Most all of us had combat experience and were aware of the crucial need of great leadership at the NCO and officer level. That awareness led to outstanding periods of dialogue and a sharing of experience, which in turn abounded in richness and growth for all of us. What an experience! Truly it was a walk with heroes and wise leaders.

One great opportunity after another developed during this year at C&GSC, including assisting area congregations and parishes that happened to be without a pastor. We were also able to assist at the Post Chapel and Memorial Chapel, which were nerve centers for the community.

All was not labor intensive, however. Our social life was top drawer and sizzled with newness and exciting friendships. This is not to indicate that they were all new friends. On pastoral staff, for example, was Chaplain LeRoy Ness, a seminary friend who was present at our first duty station, Ft. Campbell, Kentucky, and a running companion and confidant of long standing.

Another longtime friend was Don Adicks. Serving on the C&GSC Staff, this great chaplain and leader is a powerful preacher/proclaimer/pastor/friend par excellence.

And, there were sports. The 23rd Section softball team became one of the best for the year. It was fun-filled and much enjoyed by ole "Ish," as I had played much baseball while in high school and in American Legion leagues. I was invited to play (at farm team level) professional baseball as a catcher and long ball hitter, fresh out of high school—oh well!

Section 23 also was home to a new Korean friend, Major Kim Jin Young, an unmistakable leader, who shall be mentioned in a later chapter with a bit more detail.

During this memorable year at C&GSC, the Vietnam War ended. There was much joy and much regret. Much more could be said about this and our terrible pains with our political leadership—perhaps another book, even another author. I must say, however, it was not our military that squandered this time...this era. From my point of view, our civilian and political leadership lost verve, vision, and imagination in the decision-making process that was not nearly up to our national and expected standards. It was incumbent upon us to make all of this an earnest matter of prayer.

It's true that in our Lord, our sobs can be turned into songs! We must boldly "walk the walk" of faithfulness, and go forward with trust and buoyant faith life!

CHAPTER 12

OUR FIRST ASSIGNMENT TO TEXAS

Psalm 91:1-2. "You that live in the shelter of the Most High and lodge under the shadow of the Almighty, who say, 'The lord is my safe retreat, my God the fastness in which I trust . . .'"-NEB

Galatians 6:6. "When anyone is under instruction in faith, he should give his teacher a share of all good things he has."-NEB

In 1973, our home became Fort Hood, Texas, and the First Calvary Division as the division chaplain. We immediately fell in love with Texas and the Texas Hill Country: the bluebonnets, the Indian paint brushes and the countless other wild flowers that dominated the landscape in the spring; and the people, oh, the great and friendly Texans.

Post housing was not available, even for lieutenant colonels, so we "scratched with the chickens" for several weeks, staying at area motels—all seven of us. I checked regularly with housing, and they were not encouraging. They said, "No chance whatsoever for ten to twelve months."

One of the fine chaplains had a lovely home out by Stillhouse Lake, a beautiful setting in a wonderful rolling and rustic area. Sure enough, he received ASAP orders, and Praise God, he was most willing to rent to us. To be on the safe side, I said, "Just one more visit to post housing," and they again firmly said, "No chance at all for post housing for ten to twelve months." With that valuable information, Ann and I visited the Stillhouse Lake home. It was quite nice. We shook hands, Chaplain Bud Sparling and me, and the deal was made.

The very next day, the housing people called at the division chaplain's office and said, "We have post housing for you!" I said, "Too late!" We had shaken hands on it. They said that we were in the clear as long as there was no signed agreement and that we could walk and take the post housing. I advised that in my family a handshake is all that is needed—it is signed and sealed, the deal is done! I immediately critiqued the post housing officer in the principles of trust and honesty and truly caring for soldiers and their family.

We loved the Stillhouse Lake home. During our year there, we improved the property such as enclosing the carport, and the owner was able to receive top dollar for his investment. After a year, however, military housing did open up again for us.

Our post housing brought us back "full-bore" into the military community. As a family, we were elated. The school system we found to be excellent. Our elder son, Randy, (a strong young lineman) learned good tough football at Killeen High School. Each of our young people and young adults did well in their studies and in their social life adventures. Friendships bloomed and our family night flourished, as did our planned family devotions, singing, laughing, praying and dialogue. Our children were, indeed, maturing in all areas of life, to include the faith life of growing in grace, holiness, and wisdom.

During this special time at Fort Hood and the "First Team" (the name that General Douglas McArthur gave the First Cavalry Division), dear mother Bebe came and made her home with us as dear dad had died and gone to his promised rest in our crucified and risen Lord Jesus. She became a fully-sponsored member of our family. She was a grand encourager to our teenaged children—we were elated. Since Ann was working and Mom was a professional chef and cook, her skills were put to immediate use. We loved having Mother with us, and she loved being there. 'Twas a time of family adventure and growth.

Our family eagerly participated in post youth events and chapel. We also became associate members at Immanuel Lutheran Church in Killeen. Two of these great young people, Tim and Gracia, received confirmation and affirmation of baptism instruction from Pastor Marvin (Danny) Koenig of Immanuel Lutheran and me.

It was an exceedingly good thing for the children to hear another voice and pastor during those years of crucial instruction in the bold faith life—telling of the Lord of Lords and King of Kings—and the most blessed life He has called us to live and share. Stupendous!

A young person's courageous leadership must be shared. At our dinner hour together, a most important time for our entire family, Gracia asked a question, "Is the ground level at the foot of the cross?" I and the rest of the family answered, "Yes, Gracia, it certainly is. Do you desire to talk further on this?" We received a quiet, but sure, no. After confirmation instruction that evening, Gracia asked Pastor Koenig if she might address the church council. Pastor said, "Of course, yes, Gracia."

At the next Parish Council meeting, she was invited to address the church leadership. Gracia looked at the leadership and again asked if the ground was level at the foot of the cross? They all resoundingly said yes. She went on to ask, "Why, then, do you only have boys as acolytes (candlelighters and assistants to the pastors and lay leaders)?" This was a bold and powerful break through. She became one of the first female acolytes in that parish.

The First Team is a most distinctive, decorated, and remarkable unit, and it was a pristine assignment. What a holy and awesome privilege to have been the division chaplain/pastor for nearly two years. I was exceedingly blessed in having sure and steady NCO leaders and buoyant and talented called chaplains. The First Team more than lived up to the name given them in history.

It is always a special gift to follow strong and most able people, and that was our experience in the 1st Cavalry Division chaplain's office. When Chaplain (LTC) Don Ude went up to III Corps as deputy, he left a truly excellent and powerhouse team of champion chaplains and chaplain assistants, a first-rate Unit Ministry Team.

The division chaplain has a considerable mission as staff chaplain: coordinating and leading the preparation, training, and performance of all chaplains and chaplain assistants in the division. The division chaplain is also on the personal staff of the commanding general, and I served under two of the finest: Generals Robert Shoemaker and Julius Becton were phenomenal commanders and leaders. They were also top-drawer supporters of their entire chaplain and chaplain assistant soldiers/team.

Now Here's a Thought:
Boxing Makes Long-term Friends

One day, I met and visited with Colonel John (Jack) Woodmansee, a truly distinguished commander. Meeting with and establishing a spiritual rapport with commanders was a meaningful part of my military ministry. (Troops *do* look to their leaders).

Our meeting seemed to stir a disturbing gnawing at my memory bank: we have met before! I said nothing. We subsequently met again (over coffee in the mess hall), and it turned out that he had had the same disturbing feeling of a previous meeting. We went carefully over past assignments, to no avail.

On a subsequent meeting (again over coffee) I asked, "Where did you attend high school?" He responded quickly and with a bit of pride, "I went to Culver Military Academy in Culver, Indiana." Culver Military Academy is a tremendous eighteen-hundred-acre campus bordering on majestic Lake Maxinkuckee. That was it! The memory fog lifted for me! I vividly remembered Jack as a high-spirited student trainer/manager for one of the most outstanding boxing teams in our beloved country—along with Grant Community High, Fox Lake, Illinois (my school, of course).

With a bit of a twinkle in my eye, I asked, "Did you have a renowned, popular, and undefeated heavyweight champion by the name of Josh Reynolds?" Commander Jack stared me down for a moment and then said, "You son-of-a-gun (or something close to that), you are the one who knocked out our hero. I really wanted to hit you, I was so angry." Indeed Colonel Jack proceeded to swat me with his training towel that he happened to have with him.

I recall saying to him, "One more time with that thing, and you're next." With softened attitude, we smiled and then had a hearty laugh. It was a fond day of memory sharpening and sharing. Jack Woodmansee went on to become one of our finest commanders and senior leaders as a lieutenant general.

General Robert Shoemaker knew of my boxing background (I had held titles in the Midwest and the West Coast) and requested that I please pitch in and assist in getting some good "Smokers" or boxing bouts with and for the troops. At first the response was quite slow. The commander gave the program a real shot in the arm, however, when he announced that all boxing volunteers would get an extra day off, either a Friday or a Monday. Soldiers dearly value extra time for their own personal use and wisdom. The unit Esprit de Corps went through the roof.

Boxing is a rugged, rough, and a profound character-building sport with the object of hitting and not getting hit. I coached boxing throughout my military career and pastoral calling. It was not unusual to see troops in the chapel choir with a black eye, bent nose, or puffy lips; all for the worthy and noble sport of boxing. I was elated to assist our great command in this successful adventure—indeed for the "First Team."

The ongoing building and training of the First Team UMT was truly demanding. We emphasized soldier skills of the highest order, while at the same time we were developing the UMT in grace, holiness, and spiritual wisdom and leadership—all acutely important. We vigorously prepared for a ministry of caring for and general ministering to soldiers of all ages and ranks and their adored family members.

Each UMT became fine tuned and ready for any mission that we were called upon to carry out. The pastoral team emphasized that each chaplain and chaplain assistant was to be tenaciously and boldly who they were, in love and much, much more. It is in the "much more" that brings richness in diversity, preparation, and cooperation in one strong and pluralistic community, society, family, and individual.

The UMT made sure that all soldiers were spiritually and blessedly cared for and supported in their vital and innermost lives—their faith lives in the Lord, whether Christian, Jewish, Muslim, Buddhist, or other faith groups.

The devotional lives of the soldiers and the UMT was of the utmost importance, knowing full well that to bring soldiers and families to the living waters in our Lord, they had to drink deeply themselves. They had to overflow in God's mercy and grace in our Lord, and thanks be to God—that was the case!

Our Lord God was ever so good in lifting up new and trusted friends at Fort Hood. I met and became firm friends with one of the chaplaincy's best, Chaplain Henry Lamar Hunt. Lamar is a most gifted and authentic spiritual shepherd. He does it all in pristine form: he preaches, teaches, writes, and is a master musician. The Lord has truly blessed Lamar and his wonderful spouse Shirley.

The many Bible studies, Scripture dramas, and the sharing of the message of our Lord and Savior, and his forever love of each soldier and family member bore much fruit.

It should first be noted that we were fortunate to have the most superb noncommissioned officers: Master Sergeants John Raney and Harry Richards, and Senior Specialist Lou Guliano, leaders all.

I often share one memorable experience that I had while with the First Cavalry's chaplain section.

On one particular readiness training exercise, MSgt John Raney and I found ourselves in a posture of combat assimilation (close to the real thing). We were engaged against a highly trained and motivated aggressor force. It was an excellent training maneuver.

Early one morning (about 1 A.M. or 0100 hours), while most of our troops were sleeping, the aggressors slowly and silently penetrated our perimeter and launched a cluster of tear gas bombs into our midst. It was most effective. Our eyes burned, our noses ran, and we coughed and sputtered as we ran for our protective masks (a bit late, since we had already had a good whiff of that nasty stuff). John and I had very good training that morning, the message a clear, "Always be ready!"

John and I share a hearty laugh and nearly start coughing each time we remember this story.

Connie knows the value of a strong pastoral team

The pastoral team's authentic love for our Lord God and our fellow humankind was front and center; deeply and direly caring for the entire person, to include his/her spiritual heart and soul. All of this, coupled with their par excellence field training due to magnificent command and NCO leadership, led to sharp and fine-tuned soldier skills. The vital importance of depth and newness of life and spiritual growth was monumental to our entire UMT. The diverse chaplain team presented a broad-gauged and exciting walk with the Lord God and Savior Jesus and the powerful Holy Spirit.

All religious needs were served by our phenomenal First Team chaplains and chaplain assistants and the super lay leadership that was ever developing and utilized.

It is important to me to insert at least a partial list of the prestigious chaplains of the First Cavalry Division at that historic time, (both Catholic and Protestant): Father O'Brian, Al Lavoroni, Ed Flowers, Tommy Thompson, Charles Brinkmeyer, Jim Grace, David Bon, George B. Young, Elverice "Sonny" Davis, Del Eschlinger, Jim Needham, Dick McLean, Brent Anderson, Vern Gardai, Bob Migette, Vaughn Nesheim, and Don White. Only space limitations and a "grumpy" co-writer keep me from including a chapter on each of these vital persons.

The First Team chaplains and chaplain assistants were just that: First Team. They were leadership-gifted and committed, extraordinarily blessed at every level in the command. One of their distinctive traits as leaders was a beautiful sense of clean and honorable HUMOR! They were, as a team, strong, sturdy, tough, super-skilled, warm, and caring. They were ready for any demanding duty and mission. Wow! What an awesome honor to serve and shepherd soldiers with these titans of the faith!

CHAPTER 13

"CAMELOT" - CARLISLE BARRACKS, PENNSYLVANIA

Matthew 5:7-8. "How blest are those who show mercy; mercy shall be shown them. How blessed are those whose hearts are pure; they shall see God."-NEB

Matthew 5:13-14. "You are salt to the world. You are light for all the world."-NEB

As our tour was coming to a close at Fort Hood, the chief of chaplains, Will Hyatt, called and said, "Connie, I want to send you to Carlisle Barracks and the U.S. Army War College in Carlisle, Pennsylvania, to be the pastor/proclaimer and a resource person available for the staff and faculty." I took a deep breath and said, "The Lord leads," and gratefully thanked the chief.

With tears in our eyes, we departed from Fort Hood and the great state of Texas and the beauty of the surrounding Hill Country.

The journey to Carlisle, Pennsylvania, and to the U.S. Army War College at Carlisle Barracks was filled with newness, adventure, and history gathering for the entire Walker family. The family, coincidently, now numbered eight persons including my dear mother Bebe, who had lived with us since Dad's death (and promised rest in the Lord).

En route to Carlisle, we were captivated by many historical places and markers. The remembrance of the acts of sacrificial servanthood necessary for the building of this great nation was most moving. We drank deeply of the wonderment and beauty of our nation from state to state—Texas to Pennsylvania.

The large housing that we were assured awaited us, however, came to naught. Our new home on Marshall Ridge was nice but small for our family, but we swallowed deeply and painfully and said, "We'll make it work." We did.

As called and faithful servants of God and country, we vowed to provide more carefully and fully for those who would follow us, if it were within our power to do so. Our home was a deep nerve center of meaningful and jubilant Christian life, and like the wonderful hymn we were "On our way rejoicing!"

We loved the historic and beautiful area with gigantic hardwood trees, the Latort Creek, flowers in abundance, and the rich and ripe soil ready for our rosebush planting. As flower and garden lovers, we made it a point to garden and plant during our entire thirty-plus year adventuresome service journey.

When we arrived for duty at the War College, the commandant was (MG) Dewitt Smith. He is a wise, engaging, and most excellent communicator with a striking athletic background. He and his wife Betty were faithful in worship and support.

Our follow-on commandant was (MG) Robert Yerks, another caring and wise leader, also with a distinguished athletic history. He and Mrs. Yerks were steadfast at Catholic Mass and parish events, under the pastoral leadership of Chaplain (Fr.) Bud Mara, our most loved and honored priest.

Duty and ministry were mightily enhanced by my predecessor, Chaplain Kermit Johnson, who later became the Chief of Army Chaplains. Teammates par excellence were Chaplain/Pastor Joe Miller and Chaplain Mara, each all stars of the chaplaincy.

The leadership of the laypersons in both the Catholic and Protestant fellowships at Carlisle Barracks was of the highest order of service, phenomenal abilities, and dedication to our precious Lord, country, and family. Each area of interest and ministry moved with zest, wisdom, and spiritual growth—always with a heavy dash of joy and sound humor.

The Men of the Chapel program, under the guidance and wisdom of Colonels Ray Cook and Bill Rawlinson, overflowed with distinctive and challenging Christian events. This fellowship insured pronounced and alive godly growth in grace, holiness, and wisdom. Included in the effort were great and deep Bible studies and prayer fellowships. Vibrant prayer breakfasts were experienced regularly with powerful guest speakers.

The Men of the Chapel was a group of broad-gauged and buoyant growing Christians, preparing for demanding and vast leadership in and for our beloved country and our allies.

The Women of the Chapel, under the refined spiritual leadership of Ann Whitesel and Marty Bay, were true heralds of God. They continually met the special needs of the chapel. Their hands-on approach produced needlepoint kneelers, using blessed New and Old Testament symbols of truth telling. They visited area homes for seniors, cared for the lonely and sick with home visits, and had weekly Bible study and prayer fellowships.

The women had monthly special gatherings, using noted and gifted people to hold forth on issues of need, education, and service enterprises. They became very gifted in the serving of light and healthy lunches. They became real encouragers to their families on healthy living and robust power walking for normal strength building and prayer walking, witnessing in the community. They were true servants of the Lord.

The youth of the Chapel were ever so blessed and ever so inspired and dedicated to our Lord. They lived under the loving hand of our Father, Redeemer and Friend. Our cherished youth responded to the faithful leadership and friendship of Chaplains Mara and Miller, and later Chaplain Ford G'Segner, with magnificent spirits of newness and conviction that the Lord is Lord indeed!

Time Out for Joe Miller

Chaplain Joe Miller was a jubilant and loving pastor to our youth during their huge gatherings. His vision of ministry was, and remains to this day, vibrant and vast. Many dozens of our young people came to our Lord Jesus under his discipling and shepherding.

(*JWW note:* Joe Miller sent me enough material for a whole magazine article—perhaps another time. A few excerpts, however, are included here just to represent not only his feelings, but as an echo of the things I have heard dozens, if not hundreds, of times since we started this memoir.)

Connie Walker: A giant of a man—a jubilant Christian, a tender pastor, a joyful person, and a treasured mentor. And still my pastor.

The one person who has had the most profound influence on my profession of ministry is Chaplain Connie. I often find myself thinking, "What would Connie do in this situation?"

The all-time master of meaningful one-liners, Connie's phrases will frequently come into my mind when I am preaching, praying, or thinking. 'We thank you, God, that on that wonderful day in history you pulled off Operation Rescue and invaded the earth to bring us a new and deeper life!' 'Take two salt tablets, and drive on.' 'Okay, let's knock off the BS and bring on the Gospel.' 'Yeah, God!'

As I consider my life and career as a pastor, the days and years spent in proximity to Chaplain Connie Walker are counted as the most blessed of all. When I grow up, I want to be just like him.

When we all get to heaven, Connie Walker will be on the front lines welcoming his soldiers and their families into the presence of God saying, 'See, I told you the transportation was already laid on!'

(*JWW note*: Thank you, Joe, you saved me about a hundred pages of similar responses from so very many.)

Remarkable Family Memories

Our home was filled with teenagers during the Carlisle Barracks years, which led to some memorable events.

One night, the chapel chimes started playing loudly at 11 P.M. The military police desk sergeant called our home, and I answered the phone. The desk sergeant inquired, "Chaplain Walker, the chimes are ringing loud and clear at the chapel. Does someone have permission to do so?" I responded that the answer was no. I asked, "Sergeant, what hymn are they playing?" He said, with a chuckle, "Sir, they are not playing a hymn. They're playing 'How Dry I Am!'"

Laughing, I told the sergeant to be at ease, and that I would tend to it. Rushing to the chapel, I found a VW bug filled with several of our youth of the chapel. Two of the young folks had their heads ducked in the back seat and thought I did not see them. Who were they? The post chaplain's daughter Miriam and her best friend, Barbi Smith, the general's daughter!

I declared to the zestful young people, "If you see Miriam or Barbi, let them know their dads are seriously looking for them." The gleeful musicians quickly hurried home. Wise dialogue took place, along with a clear message of discipline. Miriam and Barbi are close friends to this day. The story of this happening still causes laughter to break forth.

The boys also had their memorable moments at Carlisle Barracks. Always energetic and zestful, Randy was a superb, strong, and quick lineman to the Carlisle High School football team. He had several Grants-in-Aid available to him for university based on his athletic prowess, but he felt he wasn't ready for advanced studies and the classroom. Randy elected instead to join the U.S. Army after graduation, and prior to his eighteenth birthday, we signed for him.

Randy left the new Ford pickup truck (that he had bought with his own money) for his parents' use during his basic training at Fort Dix, New Jersey. Randy had worked on a farm (near Newville, PA) as a dairyman during high school. Each morning and evening, he milked and cared for cows. He was very good at farming. At times he had to rush to the farm, then to school, and in the evening from football to the farm to home for family time and studies. He was careful, but too fast behind the wheel of his Ranger pickup!

One morning, I was out in his Ford Ranger, heading down a country road toward Newville, PA. I was well within the speed limit, so imagine my surprise when an officer of the law went around me with siren blaring and light spinning. I, of course, pulled over. The officer came toward the truck, beating his Smokey-the-Bear hat against his leg and with a bit of agitation said, "Randy, I thought you were getting out of my territory and joining the Army!" Looking closely, he said, "Oh, you're not Randy!" and I responded, "No, I'm his proud father."

The officer gave a laugh and said, "Sir, we love that boy, but we keep watch on him and his heavy foot heading for the farm or for school! We officers at our coffee breaks would often joke and wonder in whose territory Randy would be in today. Sir, we, too, are proud of Randy becoming a soldier."

Not wishing to leave out Tim in this stroll down memory lane, Tim and several of his friends worked out regularly at the post gymnasium in the weight room. Tim, indeed, became a seasoned and refined weight lifter, and he sure looked the strong muscular part.

One evening just after dark, the very heavy and cumbersome post artillery cannon was moved from its designated place to the pitcher's mound in the center of the baseball field, aimed at home plate!

The next morning our wise and friendly post provost marshall, LTC Burley Polk, came to the chapel and had a cup of coffee with me. He told me the story about the heavy cannon being moved to the baseball field. We laughed, then on a serious note before his departure, he said that it took some real strong persons, indeed like weight lifters, to carry out that feat. As Burly left, he added, "You know, Connie, Tim and his buddies spend a considerable amount of time in the weight room at the gym." The hint was clear.

At the dinner table that evening, I mentioned the visit by our beloved provost marshall, Burly Polk, to Tim. Surprise! Surprise! Surprise! The cannon was back in its rightful place the following morning. This teen-aged adventure still causes the family to burst forth in laughter.

Back at the Chapel

The singing of the youth was a mighty and bold fulfillment of their jubilant and victorious trust in our Lord. The youth met weekly in Bible study and prayer groups. Yes, considerable and individual disciplining took place at Carlisle Barracks.

The autumn and spring retreats at Dublin Gap were attended in huge numbers. Lay leaders were on hand to do eyeball-to-eyeball ministry both during the retreats and many months thereafter with the precious teenagers and family members of our military leaders.

Music and choir was a big part of all age groups in the Carlisle Barracks chapel family. Cornerstones of the adult choirs were Nancy Victor and Carol Turner and continued to be so long past our watch at the War College. Grand musical expressions took place in worship and informal gatherings and places of special need: retirement homes, hospitals, and schools. The choir endeavored to be the "Body of the Concerned"—truly a great mission statement of the chapel community.

The study of the Holy Scriptures (God's Word, the Holy Bible) took place in a meaningful and vigorous way. The paramount interest in Bible study was highlighted by the phenomenal "Overview of Scripture" in the Bethel Bible Study program.

The response was so great that a morning session had to be added to the large evening session—twice weekly—to that deep interest, in a year-long study program. Help was direly needed and Adis Rasmussen rose to the need and became an outstanding Bethel Bible teacher. She, as did our musicians, became a person "blessed to be a blessing."

The U.S. Army War College Memorial Chapel Center was a center in every sense of the word. The laity-led Jewish community was a thriving community, but for all special days, a Rabbi was secured and present to lead in the blessed "High Holy Days" and the most meaningful and important "Passover" was jubilantly celebrated. It was a considerable joy to participate in these vital spiritual events with the loved and honored Jewish community.

The Catholic community was large and full of life and zest in the faith. One of the giants of the U.S. military chaplaincy was the aforementioned Father Bud Mara. He was a pastor/priest without peer. He was a bold and sure witness and deep and devout spiritual leader during our years together (1975-78).

The Catholic and the Protestant folks did considerable didactic and joyful witnessing, singing, and Scripture sharing together—at dinners, fellowships, dramas for the Advent and Lenten seasons, and even special musical events. All of the enterprises of our Lord and

Savior were shared in jubilance and authentic love and caring.

We regularly brought to Carlisle Barracks special persons and leaders, military and civilian, known world wide to hold forth the Good News of the Gospel of our great God, Savior and friend. The entire post, War College student body, and staff and faculty deeply appreciated the powerful and gifted visiting spiritual leadership.

The response was at the same time magnificent and fulfilling, and indeed a host of future great military and civilian leaders were mightily made new in our Lord of Lords and deepened in spiritual and fitness. The impact of these truth-telling leaders is very alive even today.

The vigorous and vital years at Carlisle Barrack and the U.S. Army War College Chapel Center are remembered with great thanksgiving. The fantastic servants of God and the priests in the Priesthood of Believers were the monumental results of the work of the wondrous Holy Spirit and the faithful and stalwart believers at the chapel center.

Carlisle Barracks was a most awesome, demanding and inspirational and fulfilling (servanthood) tour.

CHAPTER 14

"WHERE HE LEADS ME I WILL FOLLOW"

(excerpt from a 19th century hymn—E. W. Blandly)

Matthew 6:31-33. "Do not ask anxiously, 'What are we to eat? What are we to wear?' . . . Your heavenly Father knows that you need them all."-NEB

Ephesians 6:10. "Finally then, find your strength in the Lord, in his mighty power."-NEB

Psalm 119:105. "Thy word is a lamp to guide my feet and a light on my path."-NEB

Our entire move to Korea (1978-1980), to include housing and vast pastoral ministry and mission, was dearly and deeply prepared for in earnest and heartfelt seasons of prayer and, of course, in our Lord's name. He is our Maker, Redeemer and Comforter!

It was emotionally draining to leave the energized and wondrously invigorating (pastoral/shepherding) call of Carlisle Barracks and the U.S. Army War College. We had a broad-gauged mission as pastor/chaplain to all our military and civilian friends and leaders stationed at "Camelot"—so nicknamed because it was near perfect and pristine. The additional responsibility of being a resource/support person to the highly professional and creative staff made for an ideal assignment.

Miriam, Randy, and Tim (three of our cherished and deeply loved teenagers) graduated from Carlisle High School. This added to our sense of phenomenal home and community feeling. It was an additional blessing that they excelled in student leadership, faith witness, scholarship, music, athletics, friendship, and fun.

As orders to be on our way to Korea arrived, our youngest scholar, student leader, choir member and bold gospel truth teller, Gracia, was just finishing her third year at Carlisle High. Ann and I gave her three choices: we would rent an apartment and she and Ann would remain to finish high school in that honored community; trusted and faithful families offered to take Gracia into their homes where she would become their family member for the academic senior year; or, she would come to Korea with us and have the adventure of studying and graduating from Seoul American High School. Gracia asked for time to pray about the decision, and we warmly agreed.

A week later, she bounced in the front door after school and burst forth the message, "I want to go to Korea with you and attend Seoul American!" It was a golden opportunity for adventure, newness, and witness. We were jubilant! (*JWW note:* There may be those among you who question the amount of space allocated to the children, Ann, associates, and acquaintances [peers and subordinates] in a book devoted to the life of a legend. Perhaps, these are the things that give substance and meaning to those we hold in high esteem.)

A peculiar (but true) happening in the lives of our three precious daughters: they all moved just prior to their senior years—uprooted and parted from their charming friends and most alive, active youth ministry, and the fellowship engendered through the study of the Holy Scriptures. This was so deeply intertwined in their spiritual leadership lives. Their sparkle, resiliency, and toughness were marvelous things. They continued to excel and always looked for opportunities to form new relationships. Bless each of our tremendous daughters.

My beloved mother Bebe was also with us. She had become a family dependent when Dad died in 1974. We traveled in warm clothing to Korea since our flight with Northwest was canceled due to a strike, and that meant a C-141. Flying in a C-141 was a new experience and adventure for my family.

(*CNW note:* I had flown in a C-141 on many occasions; however, this was to be one of very few times I would get back to the ground at the same time as the pilot. The C-141 had been my launchpad for hundreds of jumps at Ft. Benning, Georgia, the Airborne school, and with the 101st at Ft. Campbell, Kentucky.)

Our flight to Korea was roomy and somewhat cool and sometimes downright cold. Thankfully one of God's saints, Chaplain (Fr.) John Kowsky, had given me some warm, thick stockings to make my mother's flight more comfortable. Bless the good and godly man for his care and kindness. Actually, I found that Chaplain Kowsky was a great-hearted person, full of joy and a most charming sense of humor (even in his mighty prayers). I was his follow-on in Korea. He was a real giant in the faith and in humor.

When we arrived in Korea, we were still in our heavy clothing, of course. Wow! We were startled by the near 100-degree weather. We sweat buckets and were mighty uncomfortable. This incident gave the dear family another memorable moment.

Teammates met us at the airport and drove us to our temporary (and very hot) quarters. A blessing appeared in the form of Chaplain Joe Huseth, who brought and installed a delightful air conditioner—bless Brother Joe and his lovely wife, Elaine. We then rested well.

Chaplain Joe Huseth was a young soldier during the Korean conflict. For his courageous and life-threatening acts of heroism, he was awarded the Silver Star. As a chaplain/pastor, he was a champion servant of our Lord and a gifted proclaimer of the Good News.

The beloved Korean people were zealous and an exceedingly hard-working population in all their endeavors. They were highly motivated, bright, and attractive people, and, to me, full of authentic smiles. As time passed, friendships and warm relationships developed. A spirit of kindness prevailed. Korean students were most zealous in doing a superior job in school. They had a strong sense of their families' honor being at stake. Consequently, they worked long and hard with excellence.

The South Korean Forces were sharply disciplined and fine tuned in field training and combat readiness. To them, the taunting and belligerent North Korean military were just moments away. This gave a sense of urgency in training, preparedness, and faith decisions.

Into this challenging environment, the Walker family arrived for duty and pastoral/chaplain support, service, and friendship. Everything was seasoned in prayer.

My loved wife Ann gave daughter Gracia an extra measure of support. The youngest of the Walker clan was soon to be a student at Seoul American High School, where she did prima work as a student leader and a cross-country runner. Indeed, a champion runner.

Before I leave these reflections of family life, I must tell of one other experience concerning my dear mother. We were just a few minutes away from North Korean aircraft capabilities. With this actual threat so near by, the government housing community had periodic air raid drills and practices, particularly at night.

The sirens would blare, the alerts were sounded, and military police would come and announce (with their loud and clear sound systems) "lights out! Take cover! No smoking!"

Mother was a smoker, particularly when a bit nervous. On one occasion, she was standing by our large window, lit her cigarette just as the air raid marshall walked by. He yelled very loudly, "Lady, the one smoking, you just killed the whole neighborhood." Out went her smoke. She was shaken and distressed. She cried! And never again during an air raid practice did she ever light up.

When Mom turned eighty years old, she stopped smoking cold turkey and celebrated another half decade.

Oh, Yes . . . the Army!

A wondrous and vital mission was on the horizon. I was to be the Command Chaplain, U.S. Forces Korea, Eighth U.S. Army, United Nations Command. This was 1978-1980 in South Korea, the "Land of the Morning Calm." It was an exciting, demanding, and a prima challenging assignment, and the Lord's calling and mission.

We were called and we went. We were rooted and winged for mission possible. Holy Spirit, thank you!

A most appreciated gift and joy awaited us in Korea: General John (Jack) Vessey and dear wife Avis—friends of long standing and true, deep, buoyant spiritual wisdom and powerful leadership. Other mighty and godly leaders and teammates awaited me: Major General Bob Kingston, a true hero and leader/commander; Sergeant Major Bill Tapp, who vigorously and clearly set the tone for powerful enlisted training and readiness—a nerve center of greatness.

General Jack Vessey was and is a born patriot. He (at the earliest of years) joined the Minnesota National Guard as a young enlisted soldier. He served at each and every level of leadership rank. On the beaches of Anzio, Italy (World War II), most of the officers in his unit were seriously wounded or killed. At this urgent time, First Sergeant Jack Vessey was given a battlefield commission. I could go on and on about my dear commander, friend, and brother, and his illustrious calling and career as a Soldier's-Soldier/Commander, but I'm reminded that I must press on.

Since I "outrank" my co-writer, however, I wanted to add this: as far as I know, General Jack is the only person in American history to go from a battlefield commission to the four-star flag level of command and leadership. He retired as our distinguished Chairman of the Joint Chiefs of Staff. Phenomenal, and thanks be to God! We met regularly for a "pastoral call" and devotions in the Word of God and prayer together in our Lord's name.

During my first meeting at the head-shed (the HQ of our command), I was carefully and fully briefed by our chief of staff (MG) Bob Kingston and CSMAJ Bill Tapp—both true leaders of leaders.

The godly host of dedicated and effective chaplains and chaplain assistants was an inspiration and a powerful gift to me—and to all the many beloved soldiers, sailors, airmen, and marines of the command. Again, this whole magnificent mission and assignment was seasoned and put together with prayer, praise, and thanksgiving—yes, we were "called and sent," "rooted and winged," to do the vital enterprises of faith / Word / sacrament / ordinance / rite.

The UMT (Unit Ministry Team) was serious about this profound call to win, to hold, to develop, disciple, and support soldiers and their families in their walk with our blessed Lord. We were to bring soldiers to God and God to the soldiers and their families. Pastoring, shepherding, and mentoring are nerve centers along with authentic love for people of diverse and different backgrounds and faith groups.

This is the Great Commandment: "You shall love the Lord your God with all your heart, and with all your soul, and with all your mind; this is the great and first Commandment. And a second is like it. You shall love your neighbor as yourself." This Scripture passage encourages a tough and tender, loving faith life in action—Thanks be to God! (*JWW note:* The Korean Conflict had been over for nearly thirty years, but Connie was there to fight another war, the loss of which could have lasting and terrible consequences.)

Listen up! Be aware! The ministry in the "Land of the Morning Calm," South Korea, was heartening and terribly disheartening—jubilant and filled with hurt and sorrow.

It was a prayer life answered, as many troops and families became "new" and afresh in the Lord—recalled to the Lord—"born anew unto the Lord." Praise God!

We also painfully saw and experienced our soldiers, sailors, airmen, and marines off on "escape and evasion" from our gracious and calling Lord. There were considerable opportunities to be enticed to walk the wrong way and to sin (missing the mark for our destiny and walk with the Lord in faith and friendship). The temptations loomed in front of our people in ever so many enticing and controlling ways: in wrongful and dangerous sexual behaviors, alcoholic beverages mis-used, and greed-inspired misuse of money. These were haunting and hurting realities. It is painful for a pastor/ shepherd to see dear military persons and families hurt and limit themselves. It is painful to be aware of them losing the sense of value and how to live a noble, caring, and honorable life.

The battle for the lives of both our young and indeed our mature people was fierce and downright confronta-tional. It would at times be very direct and at times indirect. That which hurts our soldiers hurts all of us—our families and all that we hold dear.

Our pastoral team was there! We were sharing and giving clear alternative opportunities for soldiers to form personal relationships and friendships with people of deep and powerful caring—wanting only the very best for our people. The very best!

Please know that stalwart and sure action of the faith life took place in a big way, in large numbers, and, indeed, one-on-one relationships. They were relation-ships of trust and truth telling, they were challenging and captivating, leading to faithfulness. Considerable recalling to the road of righteousness and blessed for-giveness and newness was apparent. This was all taking place by the grace and mercy of our great God, our Savior, and friend—the Holy Spirit—and it took place continually.

Our soldiers, sailors, airmen, and marines are firmly loved, valued, and encouraged toward sound decision-making and choices of wisdom to enhance life and family. This whole arena and living adventure was, and is, a matter of great and continual prayer and prayer support for our cherished people serving in the military family. Prayer is mighty and, in the long run, has magnificent results and victory in the lives and homes of our honored people and our dear nation. (*JWW note:* I take the next few sentences very much to heart. Connie's direction and edification is of great import, so read well.)

This is a personal matter and a valued family matter—so leaders in the Lord, fondly and deeply encourage families to sustain and support family members in the military in most meaningful and important prayer in our winsome Lord's name and his forever invitation, "Follow Me." Prayer warriors are vitally and victoriously important in our military family and profoundly so from the home front. Bless you in so doing in faithfulness, power, and trust.

A major blessing for me was that one of my dear and trusted classmates from the Army Command and General Staff College at Ft. Leavenworth, Kansas, Kim Jin Young, had advanced from major to general grade and awaited our arrival in Korea. He met us with his warm and evangelical heart well intact. He went on to become the Korean Army's senior commander. He inspired many in the Lord with his winsome and strong leadership.

The South Korean military is vigorously outreaching and evangelical. They are super-trained by the early and the present missionaries, the many on the line, and faithful pastors. This spirit of evangelism and action is heavily practiced in the military to this very day. It was a blessing to often participate with their chaplain teams and administer holy baptism to thousands at a time. It sounds astonishing—but is very true!

After their soldiers made a commitment to the Lord
Jesus, they were and are carefully instructed in the
Word for several weeks, and some faith groups had
many months of teaching and instruction. It was a
blessed experience to see three to six thousand plus
South Korean troops become new and assured believers. Each month they have exceedingly large baptismal
services. Thanks be to God. We had a strong and healthy,
loving witness—they to us and we to them.

This relationship also opened avenues of close friendships with missionaries working faithfully amidst the
Korean people. I served side by side with a cluster of
missionaries during my watch. Maynard and Shirley
Dorow and George and Joan Riemer were truly champions of the faith, and there were many others of diverse
and rich backgrounds and convictions.

George was a splendid help and resource. He was a
senior reserve chaplain who assisted in pastoring the
troops and the command, all the while serving as missionary, teacher, proclaimer, builder, and administrator. He is the past Chancellor of Lutheran University
and Seminary. I once again must say the Dorows and
Riemers were used as mighty agents of the Lord. Many
new names were written in the "Book of Life" because
of their faithfulness while pastoring and loving in Christ's
name. We give thanks to the Lord for all of our faithful
missionary friends.

Pastoring, shepherding, and mentoring are all part
of our lifeblood and nerve center in the chaplaincy and
the Unit Ministry Team (UMT), along with the emphasis on spiritual leadership training and spiritual fitness.
We forever encouraged the pastoring and mentoring
loving spirit among our people. We indeed taught "traits
of a great mentor" and endeavored to faithfully live it
out amidst our entire UMT.

It was always key and a priority to spiritually deepen and train our chaplain leaders to "go higher and beyond the mentor" and to become a prima pastor/chaplain/shepherd par excellence.

The command chaplain's office was an expression of caring professionalism and a vibrant, vigorous sharing of clean humor, jubilance, and authentic enthusiasm captivated by our Lord's call to servanthood. Our fiscal and program leader was Chaplain (Fr.) Ray Schmidt. Father Ray also served the Catholic community wherever needs surfaced. He was loved as a family member in our home.

The personnel leaders and servants were two key Air Force chaplains: Meredith "Tommy" Thomas and Dick Sprowl. Tommy was a hearty and hard-working shepherd, friend, and humorist, and Dick was a Scripture teacher and servant of the highest order. Our NCOIC was Sergeant Major Hannibal Jones, a multi-talented leader of his team of young professionals.

The Lutheran Bishop of South Korea, Ji Won Sang, became our chaplain/pastor to the sharp and trusted KATUSA soldiers. They were the Korean Augmentation to the United States Army. Bishop Ji's evangelical and caring ministry was monumentally important. Over the years, many hundreds of KATUSA soldiers came to our Lord Jesus and were carefully instructed in the Word of God and then baptized as Christian disciples and disciple makers.

Our team traveled the length and breath of South Korea, checking and training in the realm of readiness and sharpness. We had a real sense of serving and caring, endeavoring to be professionals and friends. We remained true to the adage that a friend is one who goes around saying all kinds of nice things about you, behind your back.

Taegu, Korea was the assignment area for another distinctive leader. CSMG Dick Hendrickson, from the great state of Minnesota, was a special blessing and friend, and soldiers were mightily cared for under his leadership.

Dick was an outstanding marksman and periodically sent us a whole cooler full of harvested pheasants. Ann and I would invite our chaplain team and neighbors for pheasant and wild rice. It was delicious beyond description!

The centerpiece of SGM Dick Hendrickson's life is his deep relationship with our Lord Jesus. To this day, he is a bold witness and a serious servant with the Gideons.

I was further elated to have one of the very brightest chaplains in the corps as the Yongson Garrison Chaplain. Chaplain (Col.) John Logan's masterful and sure wisdom and deep spirit was forever a profound and welcome assistance in our wonderful, demanding, and vast mission.

The chaplain leadership in the 2nd Infantry Division on the DMZ was of the Army's very best. That was true both before and after Chaplain Al Brough and Chaplain Dick Martin went on to become our chaplain leaders of the highest order. Either could have easily become our chief of chaplains. They were that outstanding. They are living evidence of the principle: The mentor works hard to have his/her people to go beyond the mentor. It was my joy to work under the leadership and pastoring of Dick Martin later in Europe. Tremendous!

In the Yongsan command and Garrison area, we had mighty and gifted chaplain teams. They were much about their Father's business. Chaplain John Schumacher did dedicated pastoral proclaiming, preaching, and teaching work. He loved soldiers in a real servanthood way. Much new life in our Lord took place, as it did in the 2nd Division and the entire command. *Wunderbar!*

A Change at the Top

During our second year, Gen. John Wickham was the follow-on to General "Jack" Vessey. While General "Jack" went on to fry bigger fish, General Wickham gave broad-gauged and refined leadership. He and Mrs. Wickham were faithful in attending South Post Chapel, hearing and sharing the Word of our Lord under the grand pastoring of Chaplain John Schumacher.

Indeed the soldiers and families and the entire command were blessed with strong pastoral/shepherding support and UMT leadership. Each chaplain and chaplain assistant served with honor, wisdom, and faithfulness during our watch. Truly, it can be said that we took good care of our serving, faithful, and creative people. By the same token, we took good care of those who did not live, practice, or travel on the "high road" of witness and stalwartness in the Lord.

The Jewish chaplains during my watch were strong, faithful, joy sharing, professional spirited, and looked to the care and keeping of our soldiers and families and also the civilian community in the Seoul area and beyond. Our caring rabbis were two highly motivated chaplains: Avi Weiss and Ken Leinwand. They were solid team members who loved soldiers and their beloved families. Both of these fine chaplain/rabbis have excelled in demanding and strategic leadership assignments in the chaplain corps. May the Lord God bless them and their people in abundance!

A key area for our soldiers and command and the UMT was the retreat center at Yongsan. This heart-warming retreat place was a nerve center of training, strengthening, and prayerful deepening of our soldiers and families. It was a place Texans would call an ideal kickback citadel—for rest and recreation and re-creation in the Lord.

Chaplains Hoh and Thorp and their excellent team did considerable work in doing and caring for the troops. Special emphasis and care was given to the single soldier and his/her needs at a buoyant place of rest. There was recreation, prayer, fun, and great chow— food of four-star hotel quality!

The retreat center was open to all faith groups for denominational retreats, marriage enrichment, youth events, stress management, prayer retreats, and many Bible study/spiritual growth encounters and similar gatherings. It was also used in a meaningful way by units to sharpen leadership and communication skills as well as for noncommissioned and commissioned officer training and professional development.

The primary thrust, however, was the teaching and the studying of the Word of God: Bible and prayer adventure, retreats, spiritual fitness training, and building traits of great mentorship. We were always on the mission to train and prepare soldiers to be first rate and convinced lay leaders in the chapel community.

We trained a host of folks to return to their home church and parishes to be leaders for the Lord. Disciplining and disciple training and one-on-one training in the Lord and all His enterprises were always the keys. We forever encouraged our beloved soldiers to grow in grace, holiness, and wisdom as lay leaders, not only at the retreat, but wherever they were serving the Lord, our country, and their families.

Some Reiterations, Reflections,
and Another Farewell

The retreat center was an inspirational "hilltop" set aside for the entire military and support community for lives of prayer, praise, thanksgiving, and service. I deeply rejoice for all the great spiritual adventures by the chaplaincy team to our honored and loved people, of all ages and rank—and their dear families.

The retreat center had a most splendid reputation for the finest of food preparation (and big-time tasty) in the whole area. Troops flocked to the center for its great cuisine, atmosphere, and friendly style. A true feeding of the body and spiritual heart would take place and also a challenging environment to the creative, caring, and thinking person. Wow!

It was and is a special place for soldiers and families to be recreated, renewed, and reinforced to live the honorable and noble life and prepare for magnificent lay leadership and witness. It was a place of laughter and humor sharing, music, and dramatic presentations (such as the Covenant Players and the master Christian dramatist, Frank Roughton Harvey). It was real to life and packed with meaning and purpose-filled living.

The 1978-1980 assignment and mission was a dynamic, grace-filled and purpose-filled experience in pastoring, shepherding, mentoring, and loving ministry. Buoyant pastoral opportunities grew and surfaced each day. I traveled throughout the country giving prayer breakfasts and luncheons and doing mini-retreats and training sessions on the urgent theme "Traits of a great leader and mentor" to the UMT, as well as NCO and officer training.

It was wonderful—proclaiming and preaching the Good News in most all areas and units of the command.

Thanks be to God, the positive response was most heartening as the Holy Spirit mightily worked. The troops and staff and command knew that they were paramount in importance and that they were loved and honored.

Many recommitments and decisions for our Lord Jesus were boldly made, and considerable fresh thinking and renewals took place. Sparkling classes and instructions were held in preparation for holy baptism and celebration of the Lord's Supper with the people of God—our beloved soldiers and those honored family members—in that special place, "The Land of the Morning Calm."

A last reflection: How very blessed is the "call" to be a chaplain—a pastor—a shepherd to our soldiers of all ages and all ranks and their cherished families.

Thanks be to God, and to God be the glory! Amen.

CHAPTER 15

"O MIGHTY GOD, WHEN I BEHOLD THE WONDER"

-Carl Gustaf Boberg (Swedish melody)

Jeremiah 31:33. "But this is the covenant which I will make with Israel after those days, says the Lord; I will set my law within them and write it on their hearts; I will become their God, and they my people."-NEB

Hebrews 13:8. "Jesus Christ is the same yesterday, today and forever."-NEB

We were most impressed and inspired as we arrived at, and then claimed, our new home at Fort Sill, Oklahoma (The Home of the U.S. Army Artillery). Here we would have another broad-gauged mission.

The majesty of the early morning sunrises and the evening sunsets in Oklahoma filled us with awe and thanksgiving. Add to this wonder our regular visits to the nearby Wildlife Refuge and all the wild game— deer, elk, turkey, as well as large herds of buffalo and Texas longhorn herds—and there is little wonder that our family was truly captivated by the environment and this historic Army post.

These blessings gave us monumental opportunities to celebrate our gracious Creator's magnificent handiwork with gleefulness, wonderment, and family fun.

Mount Scott, in the midst of the refuge, gave a particularly panoramic view of the entire area. This inspiring setting was often used by our soldiers on spiritual prayer walks and retreats; sometimes in groups, sometimes as families, and often for personal solitary devotions. The refuge area was also used by both small and large groups for professional training, leadership development, and spiritual fitness events. Despite all of these captivating sites, we had to prepare ourselves for some serious mid-afternoon summer heat as we jubilantly moved into our new home in the historic and stately "Quad" at Fort Sill.

These large and distinctive quarters were built by the famous and highly-decorated African-American "Buffalo Soldiers" of the 10th Cavalry. These talented, fierce Army warriors of the plains did an excellent building job on the quarters (Motto: "Ready and Forward, We can, We will!"). My family noted that the soldiers had used cut rocks and stones from the local quarry. Fabulous!

The splendid years at Ft. Sill were blessed with creative and clear command and staff and noncommissioned officers (of the highest quality), soldiers' support with encouragement and participation in the total worship and faith life at the installation. Of particular note in this regard: Major General and Mrs. Ed Dinges and Major General and Mrs. John Crosby, along with all of their senior command and staff and all senior noncommissioned officers, were superb leaders and supporters of our soldiers and their family members.

The chaplain section's mission statement was precise and far-reaching. It read:

"General: To provide a total ministry to enable the Grace of God to be realized in the life experience of all people. This includes the entire United States Army Field Artillery Center and Fort Sill community so that people will be empowered (in their journey of life and covenant faith) to develop a caring community through effective leadership and management of available spiritual, human, physical, and fiscal resources.

"Specific: To win, sustain, and disciple soldiers (of all ages and ranks) and their families into a covenant community of faith and purpose. The Post Chaplain is the personal and special Staff Officer responsible for directing and coordinating for the Post Commander, all religious activities and their support within the command."

The Fort Sill pastoral/shepherding mission was exciting, urgent, and packed with meaning, purpose, and grace. The pastoring and caring for soldiers and their families remained of primary concern—always and forever.

Our young soldiers had come to us from all over the United States and elsewhere and from all walks of life and at all skill levels. Parents and families trusted us with their cherished loved ones. We endeavored to strengthen and enhance that trust beyond the soldiers' and their family members' fondest dreams and hopes. It became ever so clear that soldiers knew of their great value and their absolute worth and, indeed, knew that they were important, loved, and honored. At the same time, soldiers realized that discipline and hard work were expected as part of their lives. Motivation and leadership were created and became part of the soldiers' lifestyle.

Training was hard and exceedingly valuable to preserve the lives of oneself and all those around and close-by. Amidst all the determined and life-saving training, soldiers and their families were provided with the best of medical care and keeping. The professional and technical skills at the Army hospital were top drawer.

During this time frame, a most nurturing chaplain, Vaughn Nesheim, gave grand pastoral care to soldiers and families, and hospital staff and their families alike. In fact, the entire chaplain team, that is to say, the Unit Ministry Team, was an extraordinary and gifted group of chaplain/pastors and chaplain assistants. They were persons of spiritual depth, love, wisdom, and prayer. They had the gift of noble and fun-loving humor.

During our watch (1980-1984), we were blessed with a host of strong pastors/leaders in the III Corps Artillery, a true succession of staff chaplains who were championing the pastoral chaplaincy: Chaplains Chet Steffy, Bill Harbor, and Herman Kinkaid. They were excellent pastors and mentors to our younger chaplains and assistants. We had an astounding group of young, super teammates—full of spiritual zest and balance, along with refined communication skills and great hearts for our Lord's calling.

I called this fantastic group of younger chaplains and growing leaders, my "Pups." Super they were, and the name "Pups" has stuck for the many fruitful years of pastoring and mentoring. We remain together in prayer in our Lord and Savior's name. (*JWW note:* I have to watch Connie like a hawk. If left alone, this book would have more names than the San Antonio phone directory. He just flat loves people.)

I would mention just a few of the many "Pups": Steve Heetland, Joe Miller, Gene 'Chip' Fowler, Vaughn Nesheim, Tommy Thompson, Don Troyer, Fred Carr, Dan Nagel, Neil Dennington, Elvernice "Sonny" Davis, Ed Hartman, George Johnson, Tom Taylor, Jim Little, Gary Councell, Joe Silva, Don Brown, and James Taylor and a precious host of many others. Tremendous!

Our team at the post chaplain's office was full of spark, spice, support, ability, and encouragement—and a healthy dose of humor.

Chaplain (Fr.) Alquin Greenberg was deputy as well as the senior Catholic chaplain and the clinical pastoral education leader. There were two wonderful parish priests, Ch. (Fr.) John Zagar and Ch. (Fr.) John Trapold, who pastured our large Catholic community. Chaplain Paul Schriber was the training center's wise and caring senior chaplain. They did yeoman's work in deepening and preparing our chaplains as first-class pastoral counselors, spiritual and devotional leaders, pastors and shepherds. The UMT (chaplains and chaplain assistants) became physically strong and ready for whatever the mission.

One of the key and vital areas of specialized ministry was religious education for all of our faith groups. Our very well-trained and qualified leaders in this nerve center area were two blessed and humble servants of the faith. One was Sister Marie Döebel of the Divine Providence Community, who forever prayed for each soldier and all of the folks at Ft. Sill and who was full of love and grace. May the Lord bless her forever!

On the Protestant side of our large community of the living faith was Jean Vaul, a sharp and devout Christian leader/educator. She always did magnificent and complete work for all ages of people in the body of Christ—the church! She is deep in the Lord with an aura of excitement and joy in her faithful teaching of the Word to our dear soldiers and to our senior seniors.

Jean's husband, Robert, was a commander of troops in the training center. He often invited me to take the ten- to fifteen-mile hike with the troops, which afforded a grand opportunity to be eye to eye with each soldier in the march. I had some dandy visits with each individual up and down the line, pastoring young troops in a meaningful and hands-on way. Thanks be to God, for all of our chaplains operated on that person-to-person level with our beloved soldiers.

We endeavored to have our team strong and steadfast, inside and out. They worked hard at physical and spiritual fitness—not just enough to get by at the physical training testing, but we used physical prowess as another avenue of witness and example to our soldiers.

A further note in this area: The "God Squad," as we were called, fell out on our own each day at the gymnasium, loosened up and ran to Geronimo's grave, a five-mile run. This run became a time of visiting, encouragement, storytelling, hilarity, and humor sharing. It was truly a time for team building, relational building, and joy sharing. It was very much a witness to the Ft. Sill community that the UMT took preparedness, strengthening, and readiness seriously and prayerfully.

We had three top noncommissioned officer leaders and trainers in Sergeant Major "Ace" Pinson, Sergeant Major Doug Carpenter, and Sergeant First Class George Johnson during our four-year ministry at Ft. Sill. They were informed, smooth, caring, and tough (whenever needed). George Johnson later became a great pastor and chaplain in the Texas National Guard. Hurray!

Our office and ministry was greatly blessed by two exceedingly talented secretaries. These deeply caring persons—Eva Jennings and Vivian Hendrix—were a true gift. Our office team was rounded out by the fine work of the admin/budgeting section, headed by stalwart and caring Chaplains Lowell Roddy and Nick Czark.

A symphony of gifted pastoral leadership (becoming a crescendo) pulsated throughout the post. Soldiers were deepened in the faith or became new and fresh in the Lord by being born anew in the Gospel. Mighty spiritual newness and adventures were taking place regularly; one such great spiritual event took place in the training center amidst our new trainee-soldier community. Thanks be to God!

Chaplain Jim Little was leading a service in one of our training center chapels. The troops were wall to wall and singing and praying with much feeling. Chaplain Jim's preaching was full of life. He preached the law. He preached to convict of sin. He preached the Gospel. All this he did to give newness of life in Christ Jesus. Chaplain Jim then gave an invitation (altar call) at the end of the service to accept Christ or to recommit lives to the Lord. The response was phenomenal and fifty-plus young soldiers came forward.

Chaplain Jim noticed that my son-in-law, John Marshall, (an artillery commander) and I were in the congregation. Since he was overcome by the troops' great response, he asked John (a strong lay leader) and me to come forth and assist in the laying on of hands and to welcome the troops in the name of the Lord. We also lined up the soldiers for follow-up meetings with the chaplain, preparation for holy baptism, and follow-on studies in the Bible. Tremendous! It was a true outpouring of the Holy Spirit's work.

This happening was not at all unusual, and it went on week after week in the training center and across the entire post. For this and the steady and sure day-by-day work of the Kingdom of God by the UMT at Ft. Sill, thanks be to God! Truly we were, and are, jubilant in all the commitments and renewals in the Lord.

The retreat ministry at Ft. Sill went on in a big way with each unit and each UMT. One special retreat area near Cache, Oklahoma, was put together and mentored by Chaplain Homer Kohn. This ranch retreat area was blessedly used by soldiers, couples, and families to the glory of God! We thank Homer for his wonderful Christian witness and leadership—where soldiers, in abundance, came to the Lord for the first time and many were renewed, reclaimed and redeemed at the Ranch Retreat Ministry.

Our chaplain team brought in special speakers and resource persons of national and international reputation to further challenge and lead our people to a devout and steady walk with the Lord. This ministry was carried out by each of our faith communities—Jewish, Roman Catholic, and Protestant. Our beloved soldiers and their families rejoiced.

These giants of faith were also vigorously utilized for professional training for the UMTs—NCO and officer alike. These exposures to world-class scholars were a challenge and an inspiration to read, read, read and take part in seasoned dialogue in the serious matters of the faith.

The Ft. Sill and Lawton Jewish community was ever so blessed in the pastoral ministry of Chaplains/Rabbis Hillel Smalowitz and Richard (Dick) White. Rabbi Smalowitz was the unit chaplain for the military police. It was not uncommon for him to stay with his law enforcement troops through the entire night as their chaplain and friend. He made a profound and blessed impression—post and community wide. He blessed us all with his gift of wisdom and friendship.

Rabbi Dick White was an outstanding rabbi and a super patriot. Whenever the evening bugle sounded, he would rush to an open area to faithfully and vigorously salute the colors (flag) of our nation. He was a gifted teacher of the Scripture and particularly a post and community-wide teacher of God's prayer book—the book of Psalms. He was a masterful prayer breakfast speaker and blessed us all. As a distinguished long-distance runner, Rabbi White was a bold witness to all on post who honored physical training.

From my first assignment on, it was my lifestyle and practice to have regular pastoral call time with our commander and command section. Commanders and command sergeants major were most open, delighted and ready for personal pastoring. This would include devotional time from the Holy Bible and a time in prayer together.

With any growing urgency, the commanders were eager for the chaplain/pastor to visit and brief on any need(s) of the command, and most particularly any item that affected our dear soldiers. From my point of view, our commanders and staff (to include all officers, warrant officers, and noncommissioned officers) truly and personally cared for the soldier.

A unique thing we had at Ft. Sill every Tuesday was an 06 (full colonel) luncheon. It was an "at ease" and comfortable communication and informal sharing time, as well as a time of team building and lighthearted humor.

Ft. Sill had regular unit and post-wide prayer breakfasts and luncheons for soldiers of all ages and ranks. We usually had special readings from God's Holy Word, special music and singing, a devotional, and an empowering and inspirational message. This, too, was a time of sharing, growing, humor, and laughter. We were pleased that a cluster of leaders from Lawton frequented our gatherings of prayer, praise, and thanksgiving.

Ft. Sill and Lawton have a sizeable Korean population. Two Korean pastors in the area were true teammates and assisted us greatly, professionally and culturally, as well as in matters of the faith. Pastors Ahn and Chun were blessings to us.

Ft. Sill has also been mightily blessed in the priestly ministry of the community of loving and caring Benedictines from St. Gregory's Abby in Shawnee, Oklahoma, for more than 125 years. We thank and praise God for their faithfulness in pastoring our soldiers and families in such a noble and loving way. Wow! What tenacity! There is a splendid book about their servant ministry over the many years called *Tenacious Monks* by Joseph F. Murphy.

Our thankful command presented the prestigious Aaron and Hur award on 11 July, 1981 to the St. Gregory's Abby for phenomenal and spiritual keeping of our Catholic soldiers and families over the years. They, as a religious community, truly "love the Lord their God with all their heart, soul and mind, and their neighbors as themselves."

A Blend of Mission and Family Blessings

A most dynamic and challenging ministry was with our basic and advanced artillery officers. They are strong and eager, to the person, and all exceedingly bright and full of zest and ability and leadership.

These young leaders of excellence were pastored and shepherded by a dedicated and wise cadre of chaplains and chaplain assistants. These leaders were given splendid, personal and meaningful/purposeful pastoral care, and around-the-clock support. They were given opportunities of Bible studies and prayer fellowship at the chapel and in the homes of the unit ministry team and other seriously involved lay leaders and their families.

They could attend a plethora of musical and dramatic presentations: choirs, quartets, solo opportunities, string and guitar and other instrumental efforts as an experience of the faith. The retreat ministry was offered regularly, along with visiting, dialogue, and friendship gatherings. There were spiritual fitness seminars and "Traits of a Spiritual Mentor" classes. Tremendous opportunities were and are offered to our growing leadership of the basic and advanced officer classes.

And a Bit More Personal

Our youngest daughter Gracia met and fell in love with the aforementioned Lt. John Marshall at one of the many Bible study groups. They were later married at the Ft. Sill New Post Chapel—a blessed oneness in Christ celebration.

Ft. Sill was a most memorable time for the Walker family, as our two sons and one daughter were joined in oneness in Christ marriages. During this watch, eldest son Randy and Candace (Candy)—both outstanding noncommissioned officer leaders—were married at the Ft. Sheridan Chapel in Illinois in a blessed Christian wedding.

Our second son Timothy (Tim), a strong security police commander, and Heather were blessed in a oneness in Christ marriage at the Base Chapel at Randolph Air Force Base in San Antonio, Texas. It was truly a wonderful year of joy and newness in the Lord for our family. Ann and I so thank and praise God for each of these loved and cherished ones who are faithful to their

Lord Jesus and are blessing us with many loved and precious grandchildren and great-grandchildren.

With all these special events and gifts during this timeline, Ft. Sill was a most special and delightful place and ministry for us. We ever so thankfully and prayerfully remember all our blessed younger chaplains and chaplain assistants, many of whom have gone into heavy-duty pastoral/shepherding and leadership even to this very hour. They have grown into superb pastoral giants and leaders and mentors. They were blessed to be a blessing, and that they are, worldwide. Praise God!

I am nearly overcome with joy and thanksgiving for the call to servanthood and grace-filled purpose-driven pastoral shepherding. During this magnificent era at Ft. Sill, many precious and extremely valuable new and renewed names were written in the "Book of Life" by God's great grace and mercy.

No greater joy can come to a chaplain/pastor/shepherd than to be blessed in seeing sinners experience and receive forgiveness and newness of life. This is our center, our heartbeat of jubilance and thanksgiving. Profound and unending honor and glory is due to God, the Holy Spirit, for his creative, saving, and bold action in human affairs and history. Our living God has been and is actively engaged in human history with a redemptive and grace-filled purpose.

A Shepherd's Prayer

"I thank you, Lord God, for the Exodus, the Cross and the Resurrection! Father of Mercies, we come in our Redeemer's name in bold and authentic thanksgiving as sheep of your own folds, lambs of your own flock, and sinners of your own redeeming. Thank you for being the same yesterday, today and forever, our Great God, Redeemer and Friend. Amen." We can but break out in song and praise, "My God, how wonderful Thou art!"

CHAPTER 16

"HERE I STAND, I CANNOT DO OTHERWISE."

(Speech at the Diet of Worms
—Martin Luther, April 18, 1521)

Psalm 46:1, 10-11. "God is our shelter and our refuge . . . learn that I am God. . . The Lord of Hosts is with us."-NEB

Romans 1:16. "For I am not ashamed of the Gospel. It is the saving power of God for everyone who has faith . . ."-NEB

(Excerpts of a Letter Order):

Headquarters Field Artillery Center Command, Fort Sill, Oklahoma, 73503.

Orders 76-201. Walker, Conrad N. (rank and social security number).

"You will proceed on permanent change of station with temporary duty en route as shown. Information ...Assigned to: 21st Support Command, APO New York 09325, Kaiserslautern, Germany. Reporting for duty at: Office of the Chief of Chaplains, Washington D.C. 20310, reporting date, temporary duty station: 15 July, 1984, ending on or about 19 July 1984. Purpose of temporary duty: To attend the Command Chaplain's Conference. Concurrent travel...(etc.) (*JWW note:* A very dedicated Lutheran chaplain in the land of Martin Luther. For Connie, it doesn't get much better than this.)

Our new home (1984-1987) was located in a country of beautiful, delightful, and heavily forested terrain and one that abounded in fresh and picturesque waterways. Wow! There were enticing, exciting, and encouraging walking areas everywhere and in every direction. Walking is one of our great gifts in life. For years and years, we have walked four miles per day, five or six days a week.

My beloved Lady Ann was along by my side, of course, and I can't imagine a more faithful helpmate, friend, and loving wife. Together we packed our bags, declared our farewells, arrived as a team and noted that the whole adventure had been prepared for in prayer. We arrived at Kaiserslautern as a pastoral team to support and aid our beloved soldiers and their families in every possible way.

The 21st Support Command was vast and widely spread within Europe, to include Germany, Luxembourg, Belgium, the Netherlands, and Great Britain.

Our commander was LTG John Bruen and his deputy, BG Lee Soloman. They were firm, clear and caring, truly strong, dedicated, and very honorable leaders, each displaying much zest. One of General Bruen's famous phrases was "Check, check, and check." He was right; it worked. The message was, "Follow through in all endeavors and missions." (*JWW note:* It is not surprising that this phrase excited Connie. Remember the principle that his dear dad, Don Dougal, had ingrained in his boys? "Whatever you do, do well. Whatever you start, finish.")

These command leaders and their spouses were deeply committed to our Lord and their beloved church. I regularly had devotions, pastoral calls, and prayers with each leader. They were very committed to the well being of the soldier and the family, in all vistas of their lives.

BG Soloman, an exceedingly bright and caring individual, became one of our distinguished Four Star General leaders. His follow-on as deputy was BG Gus Pegonis, another splendid leader. During General Pegoni's arrival briefing, he was advised that the command chaplain—one Connie Walker—would call on a regular basis. The pastoral call would be fifteen to thirty minutes in length. Chaplain Connie, he was told, would visit with him about any needs in the command, talk of soldiers and their special lives and their requisites, read Scripture and pray. That's it!

General Gus kindly invited me into his office on my first pastoral call. His alert aide came in, greeted me and immediately exited, and as he did, he extinguished the lights. General Gus quickly struck a match and lit two candles on the coffee table and with a broad smile said, "I used to be an altar boy in the Orthodox church." He then added, "I'm ready! Drop the Good News of God's Word on me." We celebrated life together in devotions, prayer, and thanksgiving. Tremendous!

General Gus went on to distinguished fame for his masterful leadership in "Desert Storm." He served and led ever so well that he retired as one of our senior generals.

Our follow-on commander for the 21st Support Command was LTG Kenneth Lewis. He came in with a relaxed and very informative style; however, discipline, fairness, and firmness were always in place—along with sparks of humor. He and his beloved lady were kind encouragers to the chaplain team and chapel supporters. He forever had a keen interest in the total life of our dear soldiers and looked to me (along with others on his personal and special staff) to keep him aware of any special situations to better their important lives.

Two powerful teammates and big time supporters of the pastoral ministry to the troops were our two top-drawer Command Sergeants Major Bob Guthrie and Jim Hardin. These two exceptional trainers, mentors, and vibrant leaders set the tone and theme (in action) of excellence for our soldiers, command, and staff. Both men are leaders of conviction, wisdom, and bold faith in our Lord and Savior. They are honored and admired to the highest degree. God Bless!

Each May on Memorial Day we held forth in France, where our nation's honored fighting forces fell in combat, paying the ultimate price for the people's freedom. We, from the 21st Support Command, generally traveled as a team to conduct memorial services for our fallen heroes of World Wars I and II.

Along with our soldiers, we provided most meaningful and devout services of honor, remembrance, and love. I proclaimed the message of the "Living Hope" that is ours in our blessed Lord and Redeemer.

I used the Holy Scripture recorded in I Peter 1:3-5 as our text: "Blessed be the God and Father of our Lord Jesus Christ! By his great mercy we have been born anew to a Living Hope through the resurrection of Jesus Christ from the dead and to an inheritance which is imperishable, undefiled and unfading, kept in heaven for you—you, who by God's power are guarded through faith, for a salvation ready to be revealed in the last time." The service would also be highlighted with several readings from the book of Psalms—"God's Prayer Book"—to include Psalms 23, 46, 90, 118, 121, and 130 or portions thereof.

I forever proclaimed, stressed, and centered on, "God is our refuge and strength, and very present help in time of trouble. Be still, and know that I am God." The larger message therefore was, "Let go of your concerns and trust Me!" (*JWW note:* The message Connie would then and always give, not only to his "Pups," but to all Christian pastors/chaplains—"Lift high the cross of Christ and the Resurrection.")

After the memorial service, the French community would provide a scrumptious, elegant reception for the participants, to include all of our sharp and distinguished soldiers.

While at a reception, one of the French citizens approached CSM Jim Hardin (I was standing nearby) and stated, "I would love to have a fond remembrance of this great day and this most memorable event." CSM Hardin said, "Sure thing," and proceeded to take our 21st Unit crest off of my uniform and pinned it on the Frenchman from the village. The happy fellow leaped with glee and jubilantly thanked CSM Hardin. Jim is a quick thinker (as all CSMs are) and a leader of decisive and affirming action! He is the same way to this very day. Bless him! He and his precious wife Birthe are special friends.

I feel compelled to note that the Unit Ministry Team throughout the 21st Support Command was packed with professional, pastoral, and warmly relational people. They possessed zip, zest, and a sense of humor—which means so much to me.

I should have mentioned before that I was the follow-on of a master command chaplain, Ward Hagen. It is always a special kind of gift to follow a strong, informed and caring leader like Ward.

Sergeants Major Robert Everett and Aaron Gibson were our champion NCO leaders. They, too, set the pace for godly caring and wise, steady, and motivating leadership. Our strong, bright, and Christ-caring teammates SFC John R. Leonforte and Sp5 Roxanne Miller were on a clear and vivid mission: to win, to hold and to disciple soldiers (and families) in the way of the Lord and all of the Lord's enterprises.

Servants of our Lord and Savior surfaced all around us, to include one of the Army's best Bible teachers and a mighty friend of soldiers, Chaplain Homer Kohn. Homer's follow-on was indeed one of the military's very best proclaimers/preachers and dramatists, Chaplain Tommy Thomson. Wow! How blessed can one command chaplain be?

But it didn't even pause there. Another grand and very gifted pastor/proclaimer in our command was Chaplain Chuck Adams, continually honoring, winning, and deepening soldiers in the Lord. He continues his pastoral calling to this very day as the military liaison with the International Bible Society. Blessed!

The apex of our administration and budget section was Chaplain Gene "Chip" Fowler, along with Christine Feige—champions to the bone. Chip (in the recent past) was command chaplain at Ft. Sill, Oklahoma. At the time of this writing, he was just arriving at III Corps and Ft. Hood, Texas, to become senior pastor, mentor, and teacher proclaiming the "Good News." He was there only a short time when he was assigned to, and became, our senior command chaplain in Iraq.

(*JWW note:* Looking over past chapters, Connie could have said [but didn't], "Been there, done that." I find it so very interesting just how many of Connie's "Pups" and students and follow-ons are finding themselves in the boot prints of this legendary figure.)

The excellent pastoral team of the 21st Support Command was supremely rounded out with our directors of religious education: Sister Emily Rabalais and assistant Diane Hill and Mr. Rad Reavis. All were people of mighty intercessory prayer and packed with creative wisdom in the exceedingly important areas of religious and Christian education for all ages.

They had a monumental and vital mission, and they did it ever so well for our precious soldiers and family members as well as our civil servant teammates. They traveled to every area of the command and gave training seminars for all teachers and teacher helpers. They refined the skills of all to include leaders in religious education—Jewish, Catholic and Protestant communities of faith—within the command.

Our DREs (Director of Religion Education) also sponsored drama presentations throughout the year. Our young people responded to our retreat ministry in a dynamic and cherished way, and the commitments to God's great grace were joy upon joy! Our Christian education directors were gifted, steadfast, and inspirational servants of our Lord throughout our vast area of mission.

I vividly recall long, noon-hour walks and talks in the large forests in the Kaiserslautern area with Rad Reavis, a dear brother in the Lord. He has always been a very sharp and wise Christian educator in the things of the Lord and humankind. Rad is a friend of long standing, going back to the 101st Airborne days at Ft. Campbell, Kentucky, in the early 1960s. I was blessed and deepened with his counsel and buoyant wisdom and humor. He, by the way, is also a master musician and choir director who blesses the hearts of all worship-ers. He and his loved wife Mary remain distinguished participants and indeed choral leaders with several groups, to include the International level. God bless him!

Another trusted friend I feel compelled to bring forth is Chaplain Vern Gardai. Vern was in Germany and in our command at this time and was a chaplain of refined spiritual wisdom and gifts. He has been a father confessor, listener, and spiritual director to me for many years. I thank God for him!

An overview of all our pristine pastoral and unit ministry team would, indeed, fill an entire volume in itself. For each of these chaplains and chaplain's assistants, I thank and praise God, and rejoice that they are still heralding forth the "Good News" of life. We are together in prayer.

(*JWW note:* If, dear reader, this chapter thus far has seemed a never-ending litany of individuals surrounding Connie during this assignment, you might be right. I think, however, it might be wise to remind you that Connie, like the fabled Will Rogers, "Never met a man (person) that he didn't like."

It seems to be Connie's nature to see the good, the strength, and potential in all people. He prays for his avowed enemy, he nurtures any and all that would seek counsel, and he has a lifelong mission to mentor. He is quick to laugh and is not ashamed to cry. His natural compassion has led him to know that he is "Blessed to be a Blessing," and wants all to know that our gracious Lord and Savior sees you that way, also.)

Each October/November, the United States Army European Command Chaplain sponsored a special UMT training and refining time. This session also gave each command chaplain an ideal time to meet with his/her chaplains and assistants. At that time, the primary training place was Berchtesgaden, Germany—a most charming and beautiful place near the Austrian border. Today other places are being used for conferences, seminars, and training.

The whole team was always eager and excited about this area, the training, and the renewal of friendly relationships. Half of our team would attend one week and the other half the next week, so the UMT would remain in a posture of readiness and on the line to deal with any need or emergency that might arise in the command.

Our chief or deputy chief would be present at these important training sessions, and they would also give an Army-wide briefing, so as to keep the unit ministry team informed and ready. At these training sessions, our chief of chaplains would speak and dialogue with as many of the UMT as he possibly could. They were absolutely grand encouragers and friends.

The chief or deputy would have an information, planning, and dialogue time with the command chaplains. The Army has been abundantly blessed over the years in having strong and dedicated chiefs and deputy chiefs of chaplains. They truly love the Lord and his servants "on the line"— our beloved soldiers and their families—and it can't be any better than that!

Our leadership team members were convinced persons of prayer. The magnificent tour in the 21st Support Command was a heavy traveling time for the command chaplain and team. Going to our people where they labored in the vineyard was important and took considerable time and effort. It was important to see the UMT on the line and relating to their command and cherished soldiers.

As I traveled the command, I would usually be invited to give God's message to the soldiers at a prayer breakfast or luncheon and have a mini training/dialogue session in their pastoral, shepherding areas. It was vital to walk where our people (and their soldiers) walked and relate to their joys and hurts. It was always our hope to see hurts in the process of help and healing—yes and to see sobs turn into songs.

The quality of our pastoral teams was a mighty cause to rejoice. The UMT took exceedingly good care of our soldiers and their walk with the Lord. I would generally, usually, most of the time, have a special time in Holy Scripture and prayer event together. The pastoral and relational team grew in grace, holiness, and wisdom together and endeavored to pass this spirit on to our soldiers.

A most unique and considerable gift of joy for Ann and me occurred during our watch in the 21st Support Command. Three of our leader-gifted adult sons and daughter and spouses were stationed in Germany. Highly unusual, but it joyously happened. Randy, Candy and grandchildren were stationed in Augsburg; Tim, Heather, and grandchildren were at Hahn Air Force Base; and Gracia and John were on duty in Sweinfurt, Germany. This was high adventure living for Ann and me. Joy!

The mission in and with the 21st Support Command was a blessed calling and experience of great meaning and purpose. Ann and I ended this tour in prayer, praise, and thanksgiving. Once again we burst forth in hymn and song,

"Praise God, from whom all blessings flow; Praise Him all creatures here below, Praise Him above ye heavenly hosts: Praise Father, Son, and Holy Ghost." Amen!

CHAPTER 17

FIFTH UNITED STATES ARMY
1987-1990

Psalm 90:1-2. "Lord, thou has been our refuge from generation to generation. Before the mountains were brought forth . . . from age to everlasting age, thou art God."-NEB

Isaiah 32:17. "When righteousness shall yield peace and its fruit be quietness and confidence forever."-NEB

Fort Sam Houston, Texas, is a most historic Army post. It is located in and surrounded by the charming city of San Antonio, also called the "River City" and the "Alamo City." It is truly a tremendous place to live, work, and serve our Lord, our country, and our beloved families.

It was a distinct honor and gift of God to have LTG Bill Schneider as welcoming commander and friend. He was a phenomenal and caring commander and a devout and practicing Christian leader, with great love for soldiers and his own dear family. He was a mighty witness.

It was blessing upon blessing to have deeply concerned, committed, powerfully personal, professional and godly commanders, deputy commanders, chiefs of staff, and command sergeants major and staff. This includes superstar leaders: MG Chuck Honore, MG Don Echelbarger, BG Buddy Lomax, BG Sherman Williford and Command Sergeant Major Steve Weiss, and several others, a whole host of dedicated leaders who profoundly and personally treasured and cared for soldiers and their family members.

Once more, I had the very rich and most helpful blessing to follow a friend as staff and command chaplain for the Fifth U.S. Army, Chaplain (Col.) "Whit" McMillan—one of the Corps very best. He was, and is, a pastor/shepherd of excellence. He is a most gifted teacher, trainer, proclaimer, writer, and administrator. Thanks be to God for his careful and sure leadership and mentoring. He is a Biblical scholar and a mighty person of prayer in our Savior's name.

The splendid leadership team in place at the staff chaplains' office beautifully and stalwartly enhanced the mission at Fifth Army. The team consisted of a virtual who's who in caring and wise love in the Lord leadership. I shall always cherish the support and the memories of Chaplain Bruce D. Anderson, Chaplain James Welch, SGM Frank L. Gugudan, Sgt. Patrick McCann, Spc. John B Rossi, and special secretary assistant Wilma Wright.

They were later joined by other champions, Chaplain John Andrews and SGM Gus Yelverton. Wow! How very joyous we were in having such seriously productive, professional, and loving soldiers. They were filled with the Lord's leading, mercy, and grace. Tremendous!

The mission of the Fifth U.S. Army was vast, engaging, challenging, and broad gauged. It covered many states and their National Guard soldiers and leaders, and the major U.S. Army Reserve units supporting thousands of soldiers of all ages and ranks. Readiness and training was their clarion trumpet sound and the reason for the raising of unit banners and colors.

They were a captivating group of soldiers, developing as professionals and motivated for any call that our commander-in-chief, the president of the United States, considered critical and urgent in the realm of our national interest. The host of grand soldiers in the Fifth U.S. Army prepared for the worst and hoped for the best.

Within this fine-tuned, training army, we had a most diversified and multi-skilled family of soldiers. We were a community of ordinary and extraordinary people. We had noted world scholars and rare language translators like Chaplain (Col.) Charles Hedrick. We also had one of the most gifted chaplain and chaplain assistant recruiters in our midst in the person of Chaplain (Col.) Dorsey Levell. He was without peer in recruiting. Both of these dynamic leaders hail from Springfield, Missouri.

The considerable array of skilled and multi-skilled soldiers in our units causes the mind to swim and swirl. A plethora of professions and trades were found in our symphony of soldiers in the Fifth U.S. Army. (*JWW note:* When Connie begins to "wax poetic" and "bubble" about his soldiers or anyone else, it is important to know that's what Connie Walker is all about. First, is his Lord God Almighty, next his family, next his calling, and always others. There is not a self-serving, self-centered bone to be found in his body.)

I feel compelled to list some of their vocations and abilities: educators, plumbers, media experts, carpenters, electricians, actors and artisans, cement contractors, brick layers and lumber jacks, landscapers, water works specialists, painters, doctors, nurses, dentists and dental technicians, judges, pastors, heavy equipment operators and repairmen, mechanics, engineers, postal workers, bankers, ranchers, and farmers. Truly the soldiers' skills are both astonishing and wonderful.

As finely-tuned and motivated soldiers, their theme of organization was and is: Train, train, train; Prepare, prepare, prepare; Readiness, readiness, readiness! Again, always and forever they prepare for the worst but deeply hope and pray for the best. It was a most pronounced blessing to labor, pastor, and shepherd amidst these great young Americans of diverse and multi-cultured experiences and backgrounds.

A Standout

During this era of supremely difficult training, of preparedness and readiness, our command had a most excellent trainer. He is still a pastor and mentor of the first order. He was Chaplain (Col.) George Fischer, command chaplain for the 90th ARCOM. His fantastic spirit, teaching and mentoring skills set the tone for all to emulate. He was just that good as a leader, pastor, and shepherd. We thank God for such pristine pastors.

As this memoir is written, it is still a wonder to reflect on that total soldier team. The assigned soldiers were like most American soldiers in that age group, possessing lots of HUMOR, energy, ideas, interests, skills, and good will. Laughter, storytelling, joking, game playing, and hilarity was part of their lifestyle and practice. They were/are patriots with mighty gifts and one of the true nerve centers was that HUMOR, wrapped around a sense of mission, meaning, and purpose-filled lives, to include leadership at every level. They were ever so much fun to be with, day and night.

Each early morning and each evening the unit ministry team surrounded and supported soldiers and families in grace-filled, purposeful and mighty prayer in our blessed Lord's wonderful and saving name! Joy and jubilance would burst out all over the place, as they worked hard, very hard.

In the Quadrangle (the "Quad") headquarters area, where the command and staff centered and functioned, the chaplain team would, at the behest of our commander, provide leadership and resources for the quarterly Command Prayer Breakfast. It was an inspirational and faith-formulating event and always well attended. It was frequently held at the foot of the tower at the center of the park-like grounds inside the Quad.

These outdoor gatherings were as unique as they were awe inspiring. The entire presentation would occur not only with great singing of hymns but also along with the screeching of peacocks, snorting deer, hopping rabbits, and ducks a-quacking! The Word of God was shared, prayed over, and sung in the midst of the beauty of God's creation.

One splendid prayer breakfast found our command sergeant major sitting directly under a large oak tree branch with a strutting and invigorated peacock directly over his head. I cautioned our wise CSM that this bigger-than-life peacock may indeed dump/defecate on him. He said, "Chaplain, 'fear not'! I gave the bird a direct order not to dare have droppings hit the command sergeant major." Grandly, all went well and our very fine #1 soldier left the breakfast unmarked and with a huge grin on his stalwart and commanding face.

At special times, our gifted Chaplain Bruce Anderson would play his bagpipe. He is a most talented bagpiper, as well as being a mighty proclaimer of the Good News in word and song. He would often open our early duty day playing "Amazing Grace" in the Quad at 0600, just prior to our assembling (several times a week) for physical training not far from our general's quarters at the staff post parade grounds.

Each Wednesday, over the noon hour, there was a Scripture gathering and study in the chaplains' sizable office area. It was nicely attended by military and civilian employees alike.

During the eventful years of 1987 through 1990, our fellowship studied many books of the Bible. The entire year of 1990, the book of Psalms (God's Prayer Book) was carefully studied with thanksgiving and jubilance. (*CNW note:* The word "jubilance" is as important as it is captivating, both as a word and as an experience.)

In our pastoring and shepherding, joy and eternal victory was forever shared and expressed. The Spirit of the Lord was caught as well as being taught. Joy and godly humor are real and truly authentic high adventure living. And why should they not be? Anything that we might fear has been conquered and overcome by our Lord, on the cross and with the resurrection—to include sin, death and the evil one. Hurray for God!

At this juncture, I interject an important happening in the life of a former 5th Army leader who went on to be a mover and shaker with the successful First Command organization—an educational foundation. Brigadier General Charlie Canedy is a trusted friend and one of the founding fathers and developers of the helicopter in combat—with all of its firepower and varied uses.

During this time frame, this trusted friend and hero was accosted (as a retiree) in a parking lot. Two thugs tried to mug and rob BG Charlie, who was feisty, tough and ready to do combat. He powerfully resisted until one of the thugs pulled a gun and shot him in the stomach.

Wounded, he struggled to his large and powerful auto and tried to ram them. The perpetrator's sports car barely eluded BG Charlie. He chased them, but shortly better thinking took over as he realized that he was bleeding and needed to get to Brooke Army Medical Center. The Army emergency medical team quickly did their splendid work and saved his life.

I was notified the following morning. I went to have a pastoral visit with BG Charlie, but I first checked his medical record and condition. I was startled to learn that he'd been shot through a kidney that, unbeknownst to Charlie, was cancer-ridden. On both scores, the surgery did its lifesaving work!

BG Charlie Canedy saw me coming, and as I drew near, he said, "Chaplain Connie, Halt!" I did so. Then he said, "You are coming to tell me that the Lord blessed me in a special way. You are going to tell me that I am given another opportunity to walk closer to the Lord and serve Him and His church. Is that right? Did I cover what you were going to say as my friend and chaplain?" Yes, Charlie, you covered it.

We had a delightful time in prayer and thanksgiving, rejoicing in the Lord. BG Charlie and his loving wife Vera are living out their daily grace-filled lives with the Lord Jesus and are lay leaders in the Windcrest United Methodist Church in the San Antonio area. Thanks be to God.

It was my practice as chaplain, pastor, and shepherd to move within the command and staff offices visiting and making pastoral calls throughout the HQ areas. The pastoral call and office visitation became an expectation of our people. Some visits were short, some longer, depending on the situation, needs, and requests that arose. Generally the call would consist of a warm greeting, a thought for the day, a Scripture, and at the appropriate time and place, prayer in the name of our Maker, Redeemer and Comforter.

The staff chaplain's office had a known, continuous open-door policy that strengthened and blessed soldiers, their families, and their friends. Soldiers knew that they were key, they were the center, and they were honored, loved, and valued to the nth degree.

This servanthood and shepherding style of pastoring was emulated and modeled throughout the command. The soldiers had a wise sense that they were authentically and unconditionally loved, important, and in the name of our Lord—never alone! On their best of days and their worst of days, they were given a living hope attitude and the knowledge that life has meaning, purpose, and reason as they lived their important lives together with our Lord.

Training for the entire unit ministry team was vital, covering a vast geographical area and many, many commands. Each fall season (generally in October at Fort Sam Houston) the UMT would gather for an entire duty week of training. The very best communicators and military planners, as well as trainers, pastoral leaders, medical service professionals, tacticians, administrators, and command leaders, would hold forth and train our UMT (all chaplains and chaplain assistants), as well as all directors of religious education (DREs).

We would have early morning worship and devotions—for Jewish, Catholic and Protestant gatherings—and would close with evening prayers and a hymn. Each morning at 0600 the UMT was encouraged to have physical training, a two-to-four mile run or vigorous walk. (*JWW note:* Gentle reader, by now this should not be a surprise for you. Dynamic physical training has always been an integral part of Connie's ministry.)

Indeed, our team would look forward to evening events and cultural and musical presentations, along with some fine cuisine and "sippin' and lippin' sessions." Refined friendships developed, along with storytelling and laughter. There was much good, godly hilarity together.

Our chief and deputy chief of chaplains and their NCO leadership would always be with us for our yearly UMT training. The chief of chaplains briefing team would attend and hold forth for a day of richness and the most current information from the Department of the Army and the world environment. Our chief and deputy chief would visit with as many UMT members as possible and share on a one on one, as they were able. This was inspirational and important for the entire UMT.

One of the very special treats during our annual week-long affair was to have the Fifth Army Band at our special banquet, as well as some of our training sessions. The band gave a grand gift and lift to our people along with patriotic joy and zest.

The calling and assignment to the Fifth Army demanded a considerable amount of air and ground travel to visit all of our states, major units, and training areas. The National Guard and Reserve units continually invited me and my staff to give classes and training sessions on a regular basis. Indeed we taught, spoke, and attended training throughout the vast command.

We rejoiced in the grand shepherding opportunities and being in close contact with as many of our soldiers as possible.

The Citizen Soldier

The strong chaplain/pastoral leadership throughout the National Guard and the Reserve units and commands causes one to forever hum and sing the Doxology in joyful thanksgiving.

This servanthood leadership surfaced in a powerful way as the seriousness and urgency developed in Operation Desert Shield and came to vivid fruition as Desert Storm rushed upon us. Reserve and National Guardsmen functioned extremely well in both operations. Our UMTs' stringent training paid off to the fullest. Each one is deserving of a chapter, and more, on their personal and vibrant ministry.

It was a supreme delight and thrill to periodically visit congregations and thank them for sharing their pastor to minister to our civilian soldiers in the National Guard and Reserve throughout the Fifth Army. I complimented those dear congregations for their missionary outreaching spirits and evangelical and patriotic practice and caring. I warmly advised those courageous congregations that, as they shared their pastor to serve as a chaplain, they were mightily participating in many soldiers and family members coming to the Lord Jesus and deepened in the meaningful and victorious faith life.

Congregations that shared in this vital ministry to the military were themselves deepened and developed a bold sense of being ambassadors for our Maker, Redeemer and Comforter. Thanks be to God for their vision and sense of evangelical mission.

Well Done My Good and Faithful Servant

As you deal with soldiers—as you pastor and shepherd soldiers—you are walking on the sacred and holy ground of life and opportunity. Conrad N. Walker, 2003

During the last half of my tour as the Fifth Army chaplain, I had the great opportunity to serve with another of our distinguished Army commanders, a mighty soldier and leader, Lieutenant General George R. Stotser. LTG Stotser presided over my retirement ceremony in the Headquarters Quadrangle on 26 October 1990—the culmination of thirty-three years of federal service, thirty years active duty and three years in the Reserves and Minnesota National Guard.

It was a very special day for the entire Walker and Wicinski families. The day was a beautiful south-central Texas day. As I stood at the foot of the historic Quadrangle Tower, the sun was shining and the morning was blessed with a cool breeze.

The Fifth U.S. Army Band played a medley of inspirational hymns. As General Stotser and I came forward, the band powerfully played, "A Mighty Fortress is Our God." Most fitting for a Lutheran chaplain's retirement, as Martin Luther was inspired to pen that mighty hymn based on the victorious Psalm 46!

General Stotser gave his sure, refined, kind, and encouraging remarks. He then invited me to hold forth, which I did with these words: "Thank you, General Stotser, for hosting this retirement ceremony and your kind and encouraging words. This event is very significant and important to our entire family, the Unit Ministry Team, our host of friends, and me.

"Thank you, Fifth Army Band for your considerable contribution and particularly playing the loved and cherished hymn 'A Mighty Fortress is our God.' It was a mighty and sure gift. Thank you.

"I first thank and praise God for his call to be a pastor and shepherd. I thank my beloved church and leadership for calling me to be a U.S. Army chaplain/pastor. I forever honor and thank our Maker, Redeemer and Comforter for an energetic, talented, committed and loving family.

"I particularly thank my much-loved and faithful wife Ann, as well as the children—the fruit of our great love: Beverly, Miriam, Randy, Tim and Gracia. I also recognize and thank Mother Catherine Wicinski, brothers and sisters, nieces and nephews each one—and blessed friends, for your many years of encouragement and support.

"I thank all leader soldiers: commanders, command sergeants major, soldiers of all ranks and ages and civil teammates and workers, servants all. I rejoice in the many folks from MacArthur Park Evangelical Lutheran Church, our new church home, for being here today. Tremendous!

"I profoundly thank and worship the Lord for each soldier and his/her family. You are the stalwart servants of God. I honor and love you! The soldier, the soldier, the soldier—of all ages and ranks; you are sacred Benedictions to our entire nation!

> The Lord bless you, and keep you;
> The Lord make His face to shine upon you,
> And be gracious unto you.
> The Lord lift up his countenance upon you,
> And give you peace.
> In the name of our Great God, Redeemer and Friend.
> Amen! Amen! Amen!"

CHAPTER 18

A CIVILIAN PARISH, A CIVILIAN PASTOR

Psalm 23:1-3. "The Lord is my shepherd; I shall want nothing. He makes me lie down in green pastures, and leads me besides the waters of peace; he renews life within me, and for his name's sake guides me in the right path."-NEB

II Corinthians 6:4. "As God's servants, we try to recommend ourselves in all circumstances by our steadfast endurance."-NEB

The gift of God and His magnificent call of being the command/staff chaplain for the historic, heroic and proud Fifth United States Army indeed came to an end. The answer to our deep and fervent prayers, "What and where was the Lord's leading and plan for our next mission of pastoral shepherding and caring for God's people?" came in a mighty crescendo. I received a purpose-filled call to become the senior pastor of a most challenging and exciting parish from a trusting and treasured people of God at MacArthur Park Lutheran Church and School in our new home area of San Antonio, Texas, the "Alamo City."

This most splendid and gracious call and blessing of the Lord caused me to leap with jubilance and shout praises and thanksgiving. Just imagine retiring from one monumental mission one day—and putting on the pastoral yoke (stole) of servanthood the very next day. Wow! What a delight! The Lord is good! Truly the whole happening was filled with grace upon grace. The Lord calls, He leads and we hear His words afresh, "Follow Me!" The Holy Spirit, indeed, calls, gathers, enlightens, sanctifies, and preserves each of His people in a purposeful way.

Ann and I were familiar with this outstanding parish and school, in that one of the zestful and convinced young Christian leaders, David Johnson, invited us to visit and worship with these dear people while yet serving as the Fifth Army chaplain. Also, soon thereafter, I was periodically invited to come and proclaim the "Good News," along with several other area pastors and chaplains, to include the stalwart proclaimer, teacher Chaplain Joe Garcia.

This pulpit supply was done because their precious senior pastor, George Schwanenberg, was sidelined with serious medical challenges. Pastor George and his gracious and multi-talented wife Gloria had a remarkable ministry at that special place of worship, prayer, and praise. Pastor George was the founding pastor and had been faithfully pastoring there for thirty-plus years. He was one of the very best pastors in the entire denomination.

I, once again, thanked and praised God in following such a strong, evangelical, and steady pastor, especially because I sensed that this vital and demanding call of the Lord would most likely be my last pastoral call to a parish.

What a Congregation!

Thanks be to God, the congregational leadership was serious about the basics of pastoring and shepherding together. The "priesthood of all believers" was alive and well in this place of caring ministry. Their deep prayer lives and evangelical surge and Christian education attitude was prima.

The people at MacArthur Park Lutheran were inspired by a Christian spirit of love, trust, and healthy humor. Our pastoral office and team, during those vibrant and surging evangelism years, were exceedingly fortunate and blessed by our Associate in Ministry Charlotte Berger.

Charlotte, a senior in her eighties, was a winsome witness and packed with loving power and prayer. Her steady and sure work under the Holy Spirit was a mighty ministry multiplier. Her authentic Christ-caring attitude and compassion, along with our fine visitation pastor, Les Huebner, and lay leaders brought many dozens of people of all ages to our Lord Jesus and His "Body of the Redeemed" to our church and school.

Our pastoral team was rounded out by a young and talented pastor, John Cooke, who had vast potential. His dear wife Kathy and jubilant children were a grand gift to our congregation.

Our school was a dynamic, secure and blessed service to our special "little people" and their families. The school was a citadel and fortress of education, leadership, and devotion to our Lord.

Our champion school director, Ginger Hood, along with her able assistant, Ruth Miller, provided excellence in education, sound Biblical and musical (and, oh yes, dramatic) growth of discipled, productive, and prayerful young lives. Students and parents eagerly sought to register and attend our school of excellence, at that time.

Our pastoral team (and the entire congregation) was grandly enhanced by our creative and caring secretary and administration associate, Debbie Kennedy and Carol Couffer, super servants of our Lord and humankind.

Our property manager, Pat Spickler, and teammates Ernest Charles and Charlie Casillas were special contributors for the cleanliness and care and keeping of the church and school and the grooming of the seven acres of grass, trees and flower beds. Bless them for their loving care and unique witness.

The gifted organist and children's choir director, Leigh Anne Seitter, our masterful senior choir directors, Virgil Petersen and Dale and Carla Lockett, each brought glory to God and great joy and meaning to our worshipping community.

(*JWW note:* I'll take a turn here.) There may be those of you, dear readers, who are at this point asking (as have a couple of my personal proofreaders), "Just what has any of this to do with the life of Connie Walker?" Valid question.

On more than one occasion in this collection of chapters, I have interjected several personal observations. Among those asides, I have attempted to press the fact that Connie truly loves and respects people. He seems to most cherish those who use their God-given gifts in the furthering of the ministry of Jesus Christ.

Therefore, with a never-ending commitment to the concept of shepherding, Connie never loses sight of the fact that he, and we, are "not the good, but praise God, we are the forgiven."

I would then have each of you see that, once past the uniqueness of this man, the heroics and obvious strengths, there is a very large part of his ministry that deals with the gifts and contributions made by those around him. No matter be they peers, subordinates, superiors, "Pups," mentees, assigned or volunteer, professional or laity, they are precious in the eyes of our Lord. Connie feels, therefore, that he is honor-bound to lift them up and proclaim (as Paul did to Timothy in II Timothy 2:21), " . . . a man must cleanse himself from all those evil things; then he will be fit for any honourable purpose."-NEB (*JWW note:* Back to you, Partner.)

The congregation knew full well that each person in the parish was to be a Christ-caring and compassionate servant of their Lord Jesus and to all persons. Thanks be to God, they lived in an attitude of prayer, purpose, love, witness, and servanthood. Wonderful!

How exceedingly blessed to labor (pastor and shepherd) amidst these saints—yes, saints—and sinners at the same time, but thanks be to God, *forgiven* sinners, in the reality of the cross and resurrection. The Kingdom of God enterprises abounded, indeed our Lord gave us more opportunities than time.

It was a true blessing to have, during my years as senior pastor, a succession of accomplished parish presidents and leaders: Henry Holder, Roger Buckhorn, and Bill Payne along with the wise and dedicated labors of Al Kline (church treasurer). These leaders were used in raising up a substantial symphony of buoyant laypersons, to include the sturdy Don Loomis, with considerable gifts. These devoted servants developed a vast array of strong programs.

Some examples of lay-led programs included prayer leadership, worship leaders, ushers, musicians, holy communion assistants, Men-Women-Youth of the Parish, senior ministry, study leaders and many, many others. What a blessing!

A Special Ministry

A small group was "called" for a special and urgent need in all areas of crisis ministry to be trained and prepared to lead and train other laypersons in distinctive Christian caring. Our congregation prayerfully desired to become a Stephen Ministry congregation.

The Stephen Ministry, a Christian and compassionate fellowship, was a special flame of love for our entire congregation, as well as the surrounding community.

True champions of the faith warmly volunteered for the two weeks of intensive and inspirational training by the Stephen Ministry Training Team held once a year (at that time) in San Antonio. Stephen Ministry is a captivating healing ministry empowered by the Holy Spirit.

The early-on caring and loving lay leaders and founders of the Stephen Ministry at MacArthur Lutheran Church and School were Monard and Elly Weems and Doris McDougal. They are supremely gifted servant-leaders. Two other volunteers, Steve and Linda Hammond, came forward to receive the splendid leadership training and have produced phenomenal work in serving the Lord and the Lord's people.

The interest in the thriving ministry continued to grow in numbers; dozens were carefully trained to be on-the-line as Christ-caring servants and ambassadors, inside and outside of the congregation.

The ministry provided quality Christian care giving to:

* Those experiencing great hurt in their lives.
* The lonely and discouraged.
* Those with chronic illness or disability.
* The terminally ill and their families.
* Those separated or divorced.
* The homebound, the unemployed, etc.

* Those hospitalized.

* The aging and the elderly.

* Victims of disaster.

* And the list goes on, with not only those mentioned, but also the joyous events: new marriage, new child, new opportunities etc. Truly, Stephen Ministry is the Body of the Concerned.

For those who desire to know more about the Stephen Ministry Series, a system of training, organizing and supervising laypersons to provide one on one Christian caring:

Stephen Ministries

2045 Interbelt Business Center Drive

St. Louis, MO. 63114-5765

Ph. 314-428-2600

E-mail: www.stephenministries.org

The Stephen Ministry leadership and participants at MacArthur Park Lutheran Church and School were a big part of the wise and spiritual cement that assisted in carrying the congregation through the troubled water when there was faltering pastoral leadership soon after my departure (as senior pastor) and my lead-in to the Worldwide Retreat Ministry.

Along with the meaningful Christian care giving, the congregation earnestly desired further study of the Word of God. They elected to train another host of laypersons in a broad-gauged overview study of the entire Bible. Our lay leaders selected the Bethel Bible Study Series out of Madison, Wisconsin.

The Bethel Series is a Biblical overview study that is designed for the laity and taught by the laity. The laypersons who came forth and said "Send us" for the two weeks of intensive teacher training were Ken and Valda Lingle. So off for a new adventure (with my dear "Lady

Ann" and myself, also), we went and studied and prepared to teach this disciplined overview of the Word of God.

The primary teacher was Ken Lingle, who did a masterful mission, and I was his back up. This demanding and exciting adult, two-year overview study of the Bible is designed to aid members in gaining a deeper understanding of the Old and New Testament message. It gives substantial attention to defining the radical difference between the Hebrew thought form and the Western thought form.

The creative and wise use of posters, paintings, and illustrations are an immeasurable aid, helping the student retain the things learned about God's Word. The mission of this great study is to help the laity launch into a more comprehensive study of the Holy Scriptures and to help the saints to be more productive in all of the Lord's Kingdom enterprises.

Ken did a superb job of training twelve dedicated lay leaders to be Bible teachers. The congregational phase went exceedingly well during my last year as senior pastor/shepherd.

Thanks be to God, there are many good Bible studies available to laypersons and congregations, to include the dedicated work by Harry Wendt in Minneapolis called "Crossways" and "Divine Drama." Very excellent!

Another splendid teaching of the Word of God is an in-depth study, headquartered in San Antonio, Texas, called "Bible Study Fellowship." It is a rich blessing to all participating and their family members. Any of the numerous studies that come from the Benedictines at St. John's in Collegeville, Minnesota, are of the highest order of scholarly studies of the Holy Scriptures. We praise God for these and many other studies available to our dear congregations.

The Bible study adventures opened door upon door for home visitation and pastoral calling. Home and place of work calling and visiting was very productive in our entire pastoral/shepherding ministry. We would visit about anything that was upon our parishioners' minds or concerns. We meaningfully shared in Scripture, prayer, and devotion.

This was done in addition to our regular lay-visitation, which took place within a few days after a person or family visited our congregation. It is ever so important for laypersons to make the first call after a visit to our church, and this is followed at a later time by a pastoral call.

In my entire long ministry, no matter the size of the congregation, calling and home visitation has remained profoundly important in my pastoring and shepherding style. It has been fulfilling and alive with positive results.

Certainly, the priority calling is always to those who were hospitalized. This was carefully and urgently done for all of our people in the hospital. These persons were also called on by one of our Stephen ministers.

During my watch as senior pastor, each person and family who desired a call or home visit received a visit either at the location of their choice or at their place of residence, even their place of labor. We must be aware that the environment and demands on persons and families have changed over the years.

People and families are often heavily committed and obligated during the hours of the day and often in the evenings. To make an evening call in the place of residence took planning and scheduling in both the metropolitan and rural areas; our well-motivated and friendly office and administrative assistants, Debbie Kennedy and Carol Couffer, carefully made appointments for our home pastoral calls.

Our creative pastoral team hit on the idea of early morning calls to meet some of the needs of our multi-scheduled people. A whole array of interest, fun, and opportunity surged forth as many responded in a winsome way for the early morning call in the home. Some called it "early breakfast with the pastor" or "morning coffee and devotions with the pastor," etc.

We called, upon their request, as early as 5 A.M.— their decision, their choice. It became a purposeful and joyous time as people signed up for their desired hour of visitation. My beloved Lady Ann, spouse, helpmate, and friend, came along on some of these early and bright morning adventures, and she always accompanied me if the person being visited was a single woman.

This practice was not achieved without its moments of hilarity. One dear senior person said, "Pastor, if you appear at my door prior to 10 A.M., I'll throw dishwater on you!" Her message was clear, and she indeed had her 10 A.M. pastoral call and devotions!

There was always a break in this practice on Wednesday morning during Advent and Lenten seasons, as the congregation celebrated the Holy Word of God and holy communion at 6:30 A.M. during those important weeks.

Connie Gets Involved with National Politics
—Sort of

We had kind and caring neighbors living near and around the parish, to include our warm and generous friend Tom Turner. He entertained large groups on a regular basis to include political leaders (in both major parties). Tom would get on our parish calendar well in advance of his big events. He also gave the church generous gifts each year, I might add!

He hosted Vice President Al Gore one year. The security agents visited our church and asked the administrative secretary, Debbie Kennedy, if they could place a sharpshooter on top of the Christian Education Building. She indicated that this was an unusual request, and she would have to run it by our senior pastor, Connie.

I was in my office with the door open and could not see him, but we could talk. I said, "Our confirmands periodically climb up there, thinking that I don't know—so you, too, can place a person on top." I further said, "If you injure any of our people, we will, for sure, carve our initials on your forehead." ('Twas clear and understood). Tom Turner's fine event went well without incident.

During these thrilling and important years, relational and careful instruction of the youth remained a centerpiece of teaching, sharing, and disciplining in the wondrous Word of God, Luther's Catechism, and the hymnal. The young people loved the instruction, and a considerable amount of "Good News" was written in their trusting hearts and minds. Thanks be to God!

This instruction was done one evening midweek with a Saturday morning review and makeup time. The entire confirmation group also attended a summer week of retreat, sharing in the Word of God at Bible camp in the beautiful Hill Country of Texas. Ringing laughter, joy, and Christian humor and singing would abound during our time together.

Our youth ministry was blessed by our Christ-caring Sunday school staff and teachers. We will ever be grateful for the dedicated spirit of our Sunday School Superintendent John Pomykal. I would thank you, brother John, for many years of Christ servanthood.

The counseling ministry was vital and demanding. We gave it considerable importance and care. We incorporated a strong referral system for the assurance that we met the needs of our cherished people. The primary adjunct to our staff, who rendered profound professional and Christ-care type service, was Lowell J. Grabau, M.A., LPC, psychotherapist; thank you, brother Lowell, for your supremely productive care. We thank God for all of our counselors and committed caregivers!

Early Stirrings of a New Adventure

During our senior pastoring and shepherding years of 1990-1995, I received many invites to come as retreat master throughout the U.S., Europe, and Asia. I, of course, continued to remain single minded and turned down the kind and interesting invitations. Our plate was full as senior pastor/shepherd, and we treasured and loved our people at Mac Park.

As we began our fifth year at MacArthur Park, the requests for pastoral retreats continued to mount. Ann and I seriously went to our knees in prayer in our Savior's name, once again asking the Lord for clear leading.

My body was giving signals and messages that I must lighten up a bit from our wonderful but most time-demanding call as senior pastor/shepherd. Old paratrooper injuries (after hitting the ground many hundreds of times) were seriously painful and acting up along with new and peculiar feelings in the chest and upper back area. I continued to walk three or four miles each day and watch my nourishment.

The message and leading became clear that I would continue in pastoral and teaching ministry but at a lesser pace. We were led to announce to our church leadership and congregation that on my sixty-third birthday, 2 March, 1995, I would retire from the blessed parish ministry and enter the lesser paced Worldwide Retreat Ministry. That, we did.

The treasured, trusted, and loved people at Mac-Arthur Park Lutheran gave us a grand send off and farewell. (*JWW note:* I was present at the farewell, and it was at the same time joyful and tearfully sad. In one word, it was "neat.")

We blessedly thank and praise God for our joyous and fruitful years at MacArthur Park Lutheran Church and School. The years were packed with purpose and meaning in our Lord Jesus. As we left, tears were in our hearts and eyes for those most abundant and cherished years walk alongside those trusting, loving, jubilant, and Christ-purposeful people. They, and we, were "blessed to be a blessing." We could but once again break into a mighty hymn of thanksgiving, praise and hope:

"Love divine all loves excelling, Joy of Heaven to earth come down! Fix in us thy humble dwelling, all thy faithful mercies crown. Jesus, thou art all compassion, Pure unbounded love thou art; Visit us with thy salvation, Enter every trembling heart.

Finish, then, thy new creation; Pure and spotless let us be; Let us see thy great salvation Perfectly restored in thee: Changed from glory into glory, Till in heaven we take our place, Till we cast our crowns before thee, Lost in wonder, love and praise. Amen." —Charles Wesley

(*JWW note:* Connie recognizes that the emphasis has been on lay leadership in this chapter and their empowering witness in the totality of life; and that's the way he wants it. Perhaps it's appropriate to close this chapter with one of Connie's favorite phrases, "Hurray for God!")

CHAPTER 19

LIFE! LIGHT! ZEST! PURPOSE AND MEANING! JUBILANCE IN MISSION! BLESSED TO BE BLESSINGS!

Psalm 19:14. "May all that I say and think be acceptable to thee, O Lord my rock and redeemer."-NEB

John 1:1, 14. "When all things began, the Word already was. The Word dwelt with God, and what God was, the Word was. . . . So the Word became flesh; he came to dwell among us, and we saw his glory, such glory that befits the Father's only Son, full of grace and truth."-NEB

These powerful and surging words, in part, describe the saving and sustaining work of God, the Holy Spirit, in our present and ongoing Retreat Ministry in the United States, Asia, and Europe.

All of his purposeful and winsome ways and enterprises throughout the world—and the community of the redeemed, the church—herald forth and seriously point to the events that "happened forever," the cross and the resurrection of our Lord Jesus!

The Holy Spirit nudges, urges, and calls each of us to be blessings wherever we are and in whatever we do. Each of us is called and sent, rooted, and winged to be truth tellers of the Law and Gospel and agents of our Lord's grace-filled forgiveness and renewal.

We hear anew the great commandment in the Gospel of St. Mark, the 12th chapter, and St. Matthew, the 22nd chapter, when our Lord Jesus is asked, "Which commandment is first of all?" Jesus answered, "The first is, 'Hear, O Israel, the Lord our God is the only Lord, love the Lord your God with all your heart, with all your soul, with all your mind, and all your strength.' The second is this, 'Love your neighbor as yourself; there is no other commandment greater then these.'"

Many of our hearts throb and faces flush with thanksgiving and joy as we hear, once again, this primary and blessed command. Experience and personal, national and world history, however, gives us a growing sense that this is not possible for humankind to do. And right we are! The sure and faithful purpose of God is that "all things are possible" in and through our living God. He is the "giver of life"—the Holy Spirit. He calls us, gathers us, enlightens us, and preserves and sanctifies us in his love and grace.

To love with such complete selflessness is within the living drama of the Kingdom of God. We, by God's steadfastness, mercy, and grace have been called into this blessed kingdom and discipled into this kind of love, even though it will not be completed until we see our Master face to face. We are sinners and we confess and repent of our manifold sins, and thanks be to God, there is forgiveness!

In Christ Jesus we have this kind of love for God and for our neighbors—our brothers and sisters. We are children of God, even though we do not yet love as sons and daughters. We are righteous even though sin attacks us every step of the way. We are victors even though we fail, falter, and flounder. This is the very center of our blessed assurance and salvation by GRACE, through FAITH!

It is by the winsome work of the Holy Spirit we become new persons with new beginnings of love, with new wellsprings of hope, fresh and noble stirrings for servanthood, shepherding, and discipling for our Lord God and our brothers and sisters.

We, indeed, are ministers—each one of us—and priests in the priesthood of all believers at our Lord's behest and calling.

In I Peter 2:9-10, we find one of the clear Scriptures concerning our servanthood, ministry and priesthood of all believers: "But you are a chosen people, a royal priesthood, a dedicated nation, and a people claimed by God for his own, to proclaim the triumphs of Him who has called you out of darkness into His marvelous light. You are now the people of God, who once were not his people, once outside of his mercy; you have now received his mercy."

How absolutely clear, blessed, and wonderful to hear and be called afresh to be children of God and truth tellers!

Another monumentally important teaching of God's Word concerning mission and ministry is Ephesians 4:11-22: "And these were his gifts; some to be apostles, some prophets, some evangelists, some pastors and teachers—to equip God's people for the work of his service, to the building up of the body of Christ." I would further underline the foundational "Covenant call" in Genesis 12:1-3, in summary, "Blessed to be blessings!"

These are surging and powerful words. We are all summoned and called to a creative and caring ministry. Our ongoing mission and call over the past decade has been as a retreat master. Often other requests are made of me while at a retreat location such as conducting special events or preaching and proclamations, prayer breakfasts and luncheons, leadership training, spiritual fitness training, and even participating in national and patriotic celebrations.

A Bit about Our Retreats

Our retreats cover a plethora of themes: Pastoring and Shepherding; Spiritual Fitness Training; Holy Humor; Discipling and Mentoring, etc. Requests for prayer retreats remain paramount, and we receive request upon request. We rejoice and trust in the Lord and charge on in His name and continue to give all manner of retreats.

There exists an authentic and deep hungering and thirsting for a meaningful and closer walk with the Lord and a yearning to grow in grace, holiness, and spiritual wisdom. Prayer retreats do just that in the care and continuing work of the comforter and friend—the Holy Spirit.

One of the recent past heroes of the inner disciplines of the Spirit is a Norwegian devotional writer and Biblical giant, Ole Hallesby. His book, *Prayer*, (Augsburg/Fortress Publishing) and a foreword by Richard J. Foster, is a true classic and a gem. It breathes the very spirit of prayer and issues forth a blessed life of devotion, praise, and heartfelt thanksgiving. Do purchase this treasure.

Dr. Hallesby's captivating and clear theme/message is: prayer is "helplessness," and the faithful are to simply open the door to Jesus. The vibrant words in

Revelation 3:20 is a key which opens the door into the blessed and eternal language of prayer. "Here I stand knocking at the door; if anyone hears my voice and opens the door, I will come in and sit down to supper with him and him/her with me." Dr. Hallesby further declares, "I doubt that I know of a passage in the whole Bible which throws greater light upon prayer than this one does."

Yes, to pray is to let Jesus come into our hearts. We need not meet any test, standard of holiness, godliness or saintliness before we come. He only asks that we let Him come—by the wondrous grace of God!

This prayer and devotional leader practiced what he prayed. His classes began with a half hour in prayer, on their knees. This man of God, thankfully, also had a sense of humor! Laughter was one of his shared gifts.

This classical book *Prayer* was profoundly used of the Lord in a vast way for our nation's leadership during World War II. President Franklin D. Roosevelt, who tenaciously led us through this national crisis, kept a copy of Dr. Hallesby's *Prayer* at his bedside.

The president had two copies, a paperback and a hardcover, with his initials in them. He was always ready for a steady and immediate use wherever he traveled. This devotional practice by our president inspired a deep, prayerful and Biblical spirituality to spring forth for our political and military leaders and, of course, well beyond. It was a quiet and sure renewal and revival.

The question was asked up and down our civilian and military chain of leadership, "What is the boss (president) reading?" The bold answer would come, "He is reading a devotional book called *Prayer* by Ole Hallesby." Thus, considerable devotional and prayerful reading took place by our civilian and military leaders.

This spirit of *Prayer* moved in a dynamic way during this critical time in American history. Praise God, this influential masterpiece on prayer is used on our retreats even today, along with several other splendid and pristine books.

A dear Quaker, Brother Richard J. Foster, is a sure and splendid gift to us all in his most complete writings on prayer: *Prayer—Finding the Heart's True Home* and *Celebration of Discipline*, both published by Harper Collins, as well as a cluster of his other books dealing with the inner journey and prayer. They are great books, and they are friends and helpers in our devotional and prayer lives and high adventure living.

Two other winsome resources on the devotional and prayer life that must be mentioned that are used in our prayer retreats are small but exceptionally helpful and power-packed tools: *Praying for Wholeness and Healing*, and *Prayer: Beginning Conversation with God*. Both resources are published by Augsburg and both authored by the devout and spiritually wise Pastor Richard J. Beckman.

This is hard for a lover of western boots to say, but, "Sell your boots and purchase these gems!" We will mention other very helpful books on the devotional and prayer life at the end of this book.

Now to the center of the center: Our primary source is the Holy Scriptures, the Word of God and the book of Psalms. We use several translations/versions of the Holy Scriptures, so as to more often open the streams of living water and the bread of life elements that strengthen and deepen our lives of devotion and prayer.

A sparkling and recent presentation of the entire Holy Scripture—and particularly, the book of Psalms, is by the Presbyterian Biblical scholar, Eugene H. Peterson. Truly his special gift in translation is like reading the book of Psalms for the very first and exciting time.

His translation of the first Psalm begins with a pointed and catching thrust, "How well God must like you…you thrill to Yahweh's Word…you chew the Scripture day and night," and the shepherds' Psalm 23, heralds forth, "Your beauty and love chase after me every day of my life. I'm back home in the house of Yahweh for the rest of my life." This is but a taste of the clear, rugged, and buoyant rendering of "God's Prayer Book" used at our retreats.

The great and revered evangelist, Dr. Billy Graham, speaking of the book of Psalms and the book of Proverbs declares, "By reading five (5) Psalms and one (1) chapter of Proverbs daily, you will be able to read them through each month. The Psalms will tell you how to get along with God, and the Proverbs will tell you how to get along with your fellowmen." This is tremendous pastoral and shepherding guidance to the whole people of God!

The book of Psalms is one of the favorite Scriptures for our military forces of all ranks and ages. It sustains them on good and tough days. Our armed forces feed on the Word of God, especially the Psalms of Prayer in the morning and the evening, a blessed source of strength, love and daily hope!

The World-Wide Retreat Ministry is full of life energy and challenge and is creatively demanding, but the wonder of seeing lives renewed, deepened, and charged up in our Lord Christ Jesus for servanthood and ministry is a joyous gift nearly beyond description.

A Big Bump in the Road

On 19 July, 1996 I was nearly hammered to the ground from the inside. While out on a regular four-mile (moderate-paced) walk with my daughter Miriam and her beautiful and nicely behaved golden retrievers, Sadie and Phoebe, I had a strange shortness of breath and a dull pain in the chest.

We stopped, paused awhile for the shortness of breath and chest pain to subside, and then we headed back home. I had a sensing on what was happening, and I certainly should have sat on the street curb and sent Miriam home for a vehicle, but I had too much of a tenacious spirit and bold Norwegian blood in me to back off and do the wise thing.

We slowly made our way back home. Cherished wife for life, Ann, and Miriam drove me to the emergency room at the new Brooke Army Medical Center, Ft. Sam Houston, San Antonio, Texas. It was revealed to the excellent medical team that I had major artery blockage. This was a Friday, and my very trusted doctor and friend, cardiologist Dr. James Gilman, was en route home from an out-of-town mission.

I did not want to have any surgical work done without his concurrence. He arrived and met with the medical team and the surgeons who were to do the procedure. Dr. Gilman concurred and carefully presented the surgical options to Ann and me, an angioplasty or a double bypass. Ann and I elected the bypass. I rested and prayerfully strengthened for the Monday morning surgery schedule.

22 July 1996 was a beautiful and inspiring day. Our most precious family came together and prepared me in prayer and grace-filled family love. The surgical team came and briefed me on the procedure. They finished and inquired if I had any questions. I stated that I did not, but that I wanted to make a statement, and they responded, "Yes, okay."

I declared, "You, dear doctors, are called of God to do this important work and you are very good at what you do. Do the very best that you can, and do not feel bad if this procedure does not work. Learn all that you can, and know that I fear death no more than my bed at night because of our Lord's victory on the cross and resurrection. Good 'soldier theology' is alive and well— it handles fear and gives hope because our Lord Jesus has transportation all laid on." One of the gifted doctors gleefully said, "Put him under, he won't stop preaching!"

All went exceedingly well, thanks be to God. One exception was an infection in the lower left leg where the vein was harvested but that, too, healed after some special, professional wisdom and care. A group of family and faithful friends stayed with Ann during the entire procedure. Bless all of you!

Family, friends, and pastoral visits were steady, prayerful, and quite inspirational. We joyously received prayers, anointing, laying on of hands, blessings, and the most cherished holy communion—with the blessed words of promise, "My body given for you" and "My blood shed for you." It was a true and strengthening celebration of life, now and forever.

Hospital Chaplain Mike Raymo was a daily blessing with his visiting and prayers, along with a cluster of other warriors of the faith. A visit by a friend of long standing, Chaplain David Tessman, was deeply meaningful. His pastor-father was a dear friend and fishing companion during our days with the 101st Airborne "Screaming Eagles" at Fort Campbell, Kentucky.

Another honored friend, Chaplain (Fr.) Jim Sanner, had his hip surgery at the same time that I had bypass surgery. We both prayed for one another and sent messages of encouragement and healing to each other. Joy!

Many Stephen Ministry friends called and brought encouragement and prayers, to include my co-author

J. Walker Winslow and his lovely and loved wife Iva, also a Stephen Minister. Thank you, dear ones!

After the surgery, we were ushered right into twelve weeks of cardiac rehabilitation under superb guidance. The therapists were kind and helpful, allowing my beloved Ann to attend the rehabilitation care and training with me. During this process, I was most delighted to start walking again, along with a series of strength exercises.

As the walk distance developed, slow but sure, I went from a quarter mile to a half mile—and what a celebration at one mile! From that point on, we stretched it out, slowly, until we cheerfully arrived at our regular four-mile walk.

I was jubilant! Prayer walking is part of our lifestyle and joy. Ann and I have a considerable prayer life built into our walks together each early morning and some evenings. We pray with and for each of our precious and loved family members, mentioning each of their names and also whatever is happening in their important and cherished lives—in our Lord and Savior's name!

Our walking is a special, purpose-filled and grace-filled time of prayer, praise, and thanksgiving. Our purpose (as much as possible) is to see the world's needs as Christ saw it from the cross. We pray for all kingdom events, peoples, and missions everywhere.

When we have the joy of being home after giving retreats and special missions, it is a blessing to worship at our home parish, St. Andrew Lutheran. The beloved pastors and people are resolute in the Gospel and deeply caring and welcoming. Tremendous!

Part of our treasured family study, worship, and witness is at one of the great congregations of our nation, Concordia Lutheran in San Antonio. We attend on special days and events when our grandchildren are joyously participating.

Personal Retreat Each May

For several decades, I have enjoyed a retreat with a special group of dedicated servants and truth tellers of the Law and Gospel. Each person on this retreat is a leader in their areas of work and places of servanthood unto our Lord. They are spirited, joyous, and faithful servants and priests in the Priesthood of Believers. They are expert fishermen and, thanks be to God, fishers of men and all of humankind.

Our place of retreat is on the White River near Mountain Home and Norfolk, Arkansas. Our retreat master is Dr. Oswald C. J. Hoffmann, one of the great preachers, proclaimers, and teachers of the Word of God in the world. He was used by the military all over the world as a powerful and loving proclaimer of the Gospel. He dearly and deeply loves our soldiers, sailors, airmen, marines, and Coast Guard personnel.

He served for many years as the "Lutheran Hour" speaker and is still the honorary speaker. This magnificent senior/senior citizen is still doing blessed ministry; a Biblical scholar with a deep voice that sounds like a Viking in a Norwegian fjord.

The beloved Barr family from Fort Smith, Arkansas, has grandly and generously hosted our retreat over these past decades. We thank God for the entire grace-filled family.

On this retreat journey, we also fish for trout. One scary adventure in the recent past on the White River occurred while Dr. John Drager, a refined surgical dentist from Anchorage, Alaska, was my fishing companion. We were aboard with our fishing guide in hot pursuit of rainbow trout.

Rather suddenly some wicked-looking storm clouds gathered. Lightning started dancing all over the area. John and I both shouted at our guide, "Head in! Head for shore, this storm looks and sounds dangerous." The guide responded, "No sweat, we'll be okay." We yelled again, "Head in right now!"

Our guide was slow to react. A sharp and frightening lighting bolt struck a huge cottonwood tree on the river bank next to us, and our hair actually stood on end! The tree fell right next to our boat with a big splash. Some of the branches scraped us as it floated past us, and part of the tree was still sizzling and burning.

We looked ashen and were shaken. We nearly gave our fishing guide an unauthorized swim in the White River, but wisdom prevailed even though one of our fishing friends added to the uneasiness by declaring, "Wow! You two were almost goners."

We burst forth with a prayer of thanksgiving. It was close, very close. The trauma soon turned to moments of nervous laughter. Christian hilarity had its day, and our prayer lives were increased.

Thanks be to God, our retreat ministry continues to flourish and abound. We graciously age and grow and experience Godly meaning, purpose and His presence each day. We thankfully are indeed abiding, dwelling, and living our lives together with our Lord Jesus.

I Thessalonians 5:9-11:

"For God has not destined us to the terror of judgment, but to the full attainment of salvation through our Lord Jesus Christ. He died for us so that we, awake or asleep, <u>might live in company with him</u>. Therefore hearten one another, fortify one another-as indeed you do."-NEB

We jubilantly and trustingly pray and sing:
    "God of our fathers, whose almighty hand
    leads forth in beauty all the starry band,
    of shining worlds, in splendor through the skies:
    O grateful songs, before your throne arise.
    Refresh your people on their toilsome way;
    Lead us from night to never ending day;
    Fill all our lives with heavenly love and grace,
    Until at last we meet before your face. Amen!"

A MOMENT'S RELAXATION IN A REMARKABLE SETTING

Special Prayers

During Connie's ministry, he has penned many prayers for organizations, large and small, that have been adopted as their own. I have chosen two that are very meaningful to me and to many of our dear soldiers, past and present—of all ranks and ages.—JWW

The Paratroopers Prayer

Kind Heavenly Father, our Great God who invites—"Follow Me," may we with stalwart hearts declare Thee Lord of all. We ask Thy Holy blessing to rest upon all paratroopers who are on the path to secure and sustained peace.

May we be ready at all times to boldly stand up for Thy Truth and Ways, and be steadfastly hooked up to Thy Law and Gospel.

May a primary part of our equipment be a confident faith in Thee as we stand in the door of all missions in life. May the canopy of Thy Love shield and keep us now and forever.

In the name of the Father, the Son, and the Holy Spirit. Amen.

DUSTOFF PRAYER

Kind and Merciful Heavenly Father. Thank you for "calling" and "sending" Dustoff Teams on missions of mercy, under the most hostile conditions, and to this very hour, in a deeply **D**edicated and **U**nhesitating **S**ervice **T**o **O**ur **F**ighting **F**orces of all ages and ranks.

Lord, history has us standing on the shoulders of the faithful and courageous Dustoff Teams who have gone before. Bless them forever. We follow in their stalwart leadership steps. Lord, may each of us hear afresh Your summons, "Follow Me."

Heroic cries captivate and ring in our ears, hearts and Prayers, like **"When I have your wounded..."** and even today fly on missions of mercy to Lift for Life and Hope.

Heavenly Father, we trust in Your saving and sustaining Grace, now and forever.

In the Name of our Great God, Redeemer and Holy Spirit. Amen!

23/02/03 CH Conrad (Connie) N. Walker

A CIVILIAN PARISH, BUT A SOLDIER'S HEART

THE "SKY SOLDIERS" ARE SPECIAL

A FEW YEARS BACK AT FORT HOOD

TWO PREACHERS AND A JUDGE— THE BROTHERS 3

BOB CRICK AND CONNIE— NOT JUMPING OUT OF A PLANE

ON OCCASION OF CONNIE AND ANNE'S 50TH ANNIVERSARY, WE PRESENT THE WALKER FAMILY

RECOMMENDED READING

These are but a few, but very worthwhile, resources and helping friends in our devotional and prayer growth and spiritual adventures.—CNW

1. Christensen, Bernhard, *The Inward Pilgrimage—An Intro-duction to Christian Spiritual Classics*, Minneapolis, Minnesota: Augsburg-Fortress, 1976.

2. Ofstedal, Paul, *Daily Readings from Spiritual Classics*—edited. Minneapolis, Minnesota: Augsburg-Fortress, 1990.

3. Buttrick, George Arthur, *Prayer*, New York: Abingdon-Cokesbury, 1942.

4. Merton, Thomas, *Contemplative Prayer*, New York: Doubleday, 1969.

5. Qualben, Lois, *Christ-Care*, Austin, Texas: LangMarc Publishing, 1992.

6. Qualben, James, *Christ-Care Leaders Commentary*, Austin, Texas: LangMarc Publishing, 1992.

7. Foster, Richard J. and Emilie Griffin, *Spiritual Classics*, San Francisco: Edited by Harper, 2000.

8. Foster, Richard J. and James Byron Smith, *Devotional Classics*, New York: Edited by Harper Collins, 1993.

9. Frost, Gerhard E., *Seasons of a Lifetime*, Minneapolis, Minnesota: Augsburg, 1989.

10. Frost, Gerhard E., *A Second Look*, Minneapolis, Minnesota: Winston Press, 1985.

11. Qualben, Lois, *Values Symphony*, Austin, Texas: LangMarc Publishing 1992.

ORDER BLANK

The Leapin' Deacon:

The Soldier's Chaplain

by Conrad N. Walker and

J. Walker Winslow

If this book is unavailable from your local bookstore, order directly from

LangMarc Publishing

P.O. Box 90488

Austin, Texas 78709-0488

1-800-864-1648

or from our secured website

www.langmarc.com

_____ Copies at $18.95 = _____

Texas residents add tax = _____

Shipping $2.50 for 1 book=_____

($1 each additional book)

Total amount = _____

Your name: _____

Street address: _____

City, State _____

Phone no: _____

Connie and Lady Ann

Printed in the United States
24322LVS00002B/220-246